HOW
TO BE
A GOOD
JUDGE OF
CHARACTER

HOW TO BE A GOOD JUDGE OF CHARACTER

Methods of assessing ability and personality

D Mackenzie Davey

Illustrated by
Peter Kneebone

KOGAN PAGE

The masculine pronoun has been used throughout this book. This stems from a desire to avoid ugly and cumbersome language, and no discrimination, prejudice or bias is intended.

First published in 1989 by
Kogan Page Ltd,
120 Pentonville Rd, London N1 9JN

Typeset by DP Photosetting, Aylesbury, Bucks
Printed and bound in Great Britain by Richard Clay Ltd.

British Library Cataloguing in Publication Data
Davey, D. Mackenzie (Douglas Mackenzie), 1922–
   How to be a good judge of character.
   1. Personnel. Assessment
   658.3'125

ISBN 1-85091-897-X

Contents

The Author

D. Mackenzie Davey, a Chartered Psychologist, has worked in research and management. Since about 1960 he has been working as a consultant concerned essentially with the application of psychology to industry, including advisory work in the field of training, the conduct of attitude surveys, and, most particularly, the psychological assessment of executives. He lectures and broadcasts widely and has been co-author (with P. McDonnell) of *Programmed Instruction* (IPM, 1964); *Attitude Surveys in Industry* (IPM, 1970); *How to Interview* (BIM, 1975); *How to be Interviewed* (BIM, 1980); and co-editor (with M. Harris) of *Judging People* (McGraw-Hill, 1982). He is a Fellow of the British Psychological Society and the Institute of Personnel Management.

The Illustrator

Peter Kneebone, with degrees in philosophy, politics and modern languages from Oxford University, has practised widely as a graphic designer specialising in the illustration of concepts. Among the 35 books he has illustrated are *How to Interview* and *How to Be Interviewed* by D. Mackenzie Davey and Patricia McDonnell. Clients have included the Institute of Directors, National Economic Development Office, Cambridge University Press, *Sunday Times*, *Observer*, BBC, ICI and Shell. He is past President of ICOGRADA, the International Council of Graphic Design Associations, and a Fellow of the Chartered Society of Designers and the Society of Typographic Designers. His work is exhibited and reproduced internationally.

Acknowledgements

As well as those many people mentioned in the text and in the reading lists there are some to whom special acknowledgement is due. These are the people who have helped the author in informal discussions or even through contact over the years. Plainly this list cannot be comprehensive but the following deserve special mention: Rowan Bayne, John Blomfield, Mark Cook, John Courtis, Clive Fletcher, John Handyside, Roger Holdsworth, Kate Loewenthal, Pat McDonnell, Michael Morrisby, Jane Paterson, Frank Welsh.

Also, special thanks are due to John Handslip of Lucas (now with GEC) and R. O'Callaghan of Boots who read and made helpful, constructive comments on the manuscript.

Introduction

What it's about

This book is a survey of many approaches to judging people, past and present, orthodox and unorthodox. It is an honest attempt to separate the valid techniques from the invalid and an attempt to help the reader to discriminate between the *science* and the *art* of judgement. Almost everyone is called upon to make judgements concerning people — many have to do it several times in a day. Some of these judgements are relatively unimportant, others may be momentous with long-lasting and sometimes severe consequences.

This book should give answers to such questions as:

- Is there anything in astrology?
- What can psychological tests tell me?
- How can I learn to use them?
- What about graphology?
- What is body language?
- Can I assess character from body movements?
- How do I spot the high flyer?
- What are assessment centres?
- Does an individual's background give any guidance as to how he will behave in the future?
- Are first impressions reliable?
- How should I conduct an interview?
- Have we anything to learn from the ancients on such crafts as physiognomy, phrenology, palmistry etc.?

This book will not provide all the answers but it will give some guidance on putting some of the more practical techniques into practice and offer advice on whether it is worth time investigating some of the more arcane techniques.

Who should read it?

The first group of people must be those in, or entering, fields where the judgement of people is a central part of the job. This will involve people in the whole field of human resources but especially those in

9

recruitment and staff development. While this text is not aimed at sophisticated personnel professionals, perhaps even they could learn something about the value (or otherwise) of some of the less orthodox techniques. Many personnel managers must have wondered from time to time about whether they should learn more about graphology or body language.

Secondly, the book should be valuable to less specialised managers but nevertheless those who have to make decisions about selection, promotion, transfer and the allocation of duties and responsibilities. ('Managers' here would include head teachers, professors, hospital administrators, public servants and senior members of almost any trade or profession.)

Thirdly, it should be of interest to anyone who is fascinated by human behaviour and concerned with predicting it. This may include areas over which they had no control: will X make a good captain of the national football team, will B make a good cabinet minister, will C be a good chief of police? There must be few people who do not take interest in — even pleasure from — summing people up and speculating about how they are likely to behave in a range of different situations.

What this book will not do

It will not turn readers into qualified psychologists, graphologists or astrologers. It will, however, provide them with sources of information should they wish to pursue certain studies. The book will provide further reading even for those approaches which are often dismissed as worthless.

It is the hope of the author and illustrator not only to satisfy some of the curiosity of people about human behaviour but also to leave them better informed and with a better understanding of which pointers to trust and which to ignore.

DMD

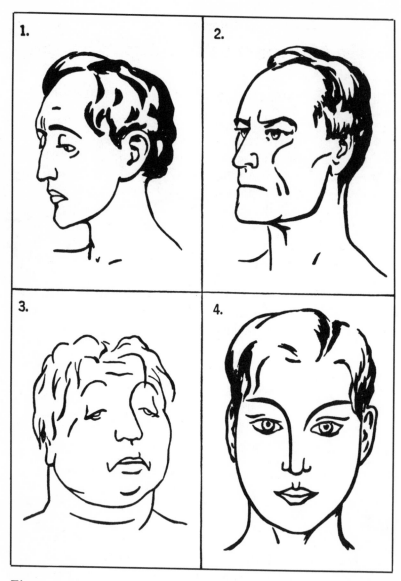

Figure 1 Physiognomic representations of the four temperaments.
1. Melancholic. 2. Choleric. 3. Phlegmatic. 4. Sanguine. (Allport, 1937)

Chapter 1
Early Approaches to Judging People

The Greeks and the concept of the humours

People have always tried to judge others. Self-defence, self-interest and curiosity all provide powerful motives for judging people: a practice which goes back at least to the Ancient Greeks. Hippocrates, the father of medicine, took up and developed the concept of *humours* (like so many ideas, his was not an original thought but had developed from ideas which related to the macrocosm — the universe — as opposed to microcosms, which are parts of the whole and have a similar structure to it). Man, it was argued, like all creation, was composed of the four elements: air, earth, fire and water. These the body received in food, which was converted in the liver to form liquid substances, the 'humours', which, in turn, corresponded to the original elements. The humours determined the temperament of the individual. Table 1 summarises this ancient thinking.

Table 1 The humours

Cosmic elements	Their properties	Corresponding humours	Corresponding temperaments
Air	Warm and moist	Blood	Sanguine
Earth	Cold and dry	Black bile	Melancholic
Fire	Warm and dry	Yellow bile	Choleric
Water	Cold and moist	Phlegm	Phlegmatic

While the specific 'humours' advanced by Hippocrates have been completely abandoned there still remains some value in the temperamental types and, even today, people who are familiar with the characteristics of the four temperaments can recognise them in drawings of the four types (see Figure 1.). Most people would see Number 1 as looking like the traditional love-sick poet who is by reputation melancholic. Number 2 is the fighter — well endowed with choler. Number 3 is sleepy, flaccid and phlegmatic, and Number 4, with his cheerful optimism, is judged sanguine.

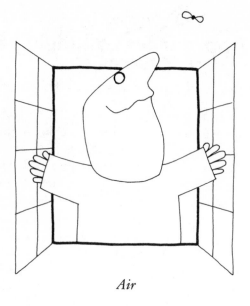

Air

Earth

Fire

Water

Professor Eysenck's detailed studies suggest two 'dimensions' of personality — introversion/extraversion, and stability/instability. The following diagram shows the relationship between ancient ideas and modern findings.

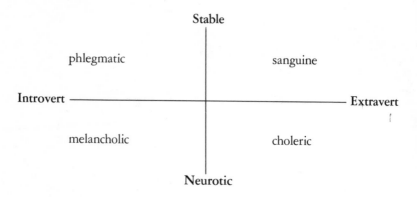

Before moving on to consider further diagnosis of personality from outward appearance (called 'physiognomy') it is worth considering another Greek — Theophrastos. He was a pupil of Aristotle who, it has been claimed, was the originator of the Greek art form of 'character writing'. Certainly he wrote some vivid portraits many of which are easily recognisable today. (One authority claims he wrote his *Characters* when he was ninety-nine years old. However, as his life dates are given by modern authorities as 372–287 BC this must be at least debatable!) Consider the Penurious Man:

> Penuriousness is economy carried beyond all measure. When his servant breaks a pot or a plate, he deducts the value from his food. If his wife drops a copper, he moves furniture, beds, chests and hunts in the curtains. He forbids anyone to pick a fig in his garden, to walk on his land, to pick up an olive or a date. He forbids his wife to lend anything — neither salt nor lamp-wick nor cinnamon nor marjoram nor meal nor garlands nor cakes for sacrifices. 'All these trifles,' he says, 'mount up in a year'.

Physiognomy

The art of physiognomy is probably as old as mankind. Aristotle — the Greeks again! — is credited with the oldest tract on the subject. One method worked on the basis of resemblances between people and

animals and assumed that they must have the same psychic qualities — a man who looks like a fox must be sly. And do we still not think of owl-like people as looking wise?

There have been several revivals of this 'art' and with it, it would appear, came mountebanks, quacks and charlatans. In the sixteenth century a law was passed to try and restrain them and again in the eighteenth century an act of parliament deemed all persons pretending to have skill in physiognomy 'rogues and vagabonds, to be publicly whipped or sent to houses of correction'. The law has its attractions but today perhaps we are a little more sensitive to the difficulties of discriminating between the charlatan and genuine professional than was the case in more robust times.

One of the great breakthroughs in organised methods of assessment came in 1775 with the publication of Lavater's prodigious work, *Essays on Physiognomy*. This was immediately successful and widely translated (there were, in fact, no less than twenty English editions over forty years after the first publication). These books were magnificently illustrated with more than eight hundred engravings, mainly by distinguished artists of the day including Fuseli and Blake, and at that time formed an essential part of any gentleman's library.

Lavater began, interestingly, by accepting the doctrines of humours. It is suggested that he had such faith in his diagnosis that, should the portrait of a great man not fit, he would have no hesitation in blaming the artist (he rejected the Gilbert Stuart painting of George Washington as historically inaccurate, since it did not follow the physiognomological requirements of a hero). Indeed, it is suggested that his descriptions of the 'military man' influenced the style and dress of soldiers for many years.

Phrenology

Following Lavater came an extraordinary American figure — Orson Squire Fowler — who by his passionate practising and teaching of phrenology created a very remarkable boom in the United States and later in Europe. Fowler, a man of great vigour, not only 'read heads' but also published books, lectured, established a museum of skulls, advocated temperance, vegetarianism, avant-garde architecture, shorthand, hydrotherapy, abolition of slavery and Equal Rights for women. He was a marriage counsellor and a pioneer in the then forbidden area

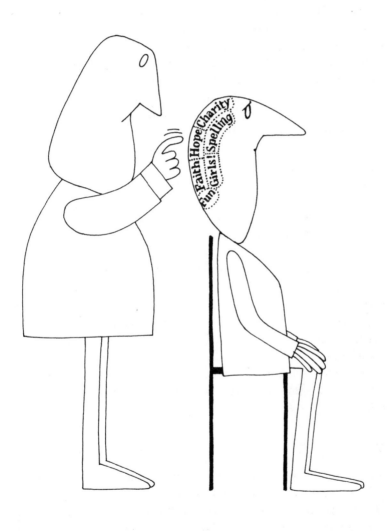

of sex education. But, while he and his associates were campaigning so vigorously, others were conducting more rigorous examinations which totally discredited phrenology by drawing attention to the fallacious hypotheses underlying the 'science'. Phrenologists believed that the brain consisted of a number of organs corresponding to the various faculties of the mind (at best, poor neurology) and that the size of the organ was a measure of its power (which is not the case), and that this size was in evidence in the 'bumps' on the skull (again, false). The old phrenological heads with their quaint descriptive terms (*amativeness, mirthfulness, alimentiveness*) are now only seen in antique shops or, as a joke, in the studies of trendy psychologists.

Writers and artists have long assumed some sort of psycho-physical relationship. Perhaps best known of these is Shakespeare who has, for example, Julius Caesar saying:

> Let me have men about me that are fat,
> Sleek-headed men, and such as sleep o' nights:
> Yond Cassius has a lean and hungry look;
> He thinks too much: such men are dangerous.
> (*Julius Caesar*, Act I, scene ii)

This was followed by scientists adopting their usual 'classification' approach: 'kinds' of plants, 'kinds' of rocks, 'kinds' of animals etc., setting up laboratories to examine 'kinds' of people. Perhaps the most distinguished of the earlier research workers was Ernst Kretshmer who observed that patients in mental hospitals with different illnesses appeared to belong to different body types. He eventually named three basic types: *pyknic* (stocky), *asthenic* (slender) and *athletic* (muscular). He also used one mixed-type category: *dysplastic* (disproportioned). Kretshmer believed that the pyknic body type was predisposed to manic depression and the asthenic to schizophrenia. Later research has provided little or no evidence to support these claims.

Kretshmer was followed by Sheldon who sought a general theory of personality and did not limit himself to psycho-pathology. He hypothesized three fundamental constitutional types: *ectomorphic* (light boned), *endomorphic* (heavy, fat) and *mezomorphic* (strong and muscular). He tended to relate these to what he believed were the three primary components of temperament: *viscerotonia* (loving, comfortable, sociable), *sematotonia* (vigorous, physical, adventurous)

and *cerevrotonia* (restrained, fearful, self-conscious). Sheldon's systematic studies appear to provide early evidence of validity but, as a unified theory of personality, it has failed.

Palmistry

As we have discussed in this chapter — and will be discussing in greater detail in Chapter 3 — there is little doubt that beliefs about people's appearance or behaviour can influence the perception of their personalities. This could be quite unfair. There is, for example, little support or evidence for the belief that a firm handshake is a sign of honesty, or that long fingers suggest an artistic temperament. (Although in one study it was found that 36 per cent of a first-year psychology class agreed that people with long fingers *are* likely to be artistic.) If such beliefs *are* held they could have real consequences, whether the belief is true or not.

The examination of the lines on the palm of the hand, with its association with booths on the pier, at first seems an unlikely field for scientific study. However, such studies have been carried out, notably by Rowan Bayne, a PhD from the University of Aberdeen, a one-time psychologist in the Civil Service and now a lecturer in psychology. He is not a man who is likely to be attracted to phoney techniques. Bayne points out that palm creases (unlike finger prints) *do* change and he has found that certain changes appear to be related to changes of personality. Although Bayne takes care to point out that many palmists (or 'chirologists' as the scientific workers prefer to be called) emphasise the holistic nature of their subject. (They argue that all hand characteristics need to be taken into account and balanced against each other before worthwhile assessments can be made.) This is probably necessary, given the complexity of personality, but can be troublesome in scientific research. For instance, the chirologists may argue that a particular strongly evident sign is not significant because it is overruled by another or by the environment in which it is found. It thus becomes all too easy for the unsuccessful prediction to be explained away and replaced with a new one.

Bayne points out that if palmistry *does* measure personality it has some special strengths as a test. Firstly, it seems likely to be a very reliable test: trained raters usually agree with each other. Secondly, the palmist's assessment should not be influenced by the candidates'

boredom, enthusiasm, suspicion etc. Thirdly, faking should not be a problem (unless, of course, such drastic measures as plastic surgery are resorted to). Finally, it should not be an expensive exercise: it should not take a trained palmist a long time to assess a candidate's suitability for, say, a high managerial post.

However, even an enthusiast such as Bayne says no more than the 'evidence of chirology as a measure of personality is by no means conclusive but worth following up'.

Astrology

Most people view this ancient study with amused scepticism, even though they may occasionally look at their horoscopes in the popular papers. Scientists, on the whole, have been mordantly severe in the rejection of astrology as a key to personality. And even most of the few committed students admit that their belief is emotionally rather than scientifically based.

In recent years, however, there have been some remarkable changes. In France, Gauquelin, formerly a sceptic, examined the planetary charts of large groups of people. In 2000 leading sportsmen he found that 21 per cent were born when Mars was just passing the ascendant, when the expected figure is 15 per cent — a statistically significant difference. This approach has been followed up in this country by Professor Eysenck and Dr Nias. There seems little doubt that some puzzling but undeniable connections exist between planetary positions and success in particular professions. It is not, it should be noted, simply enough to know one's birth sign. Indeed, the zodiac signs by themselves appear to be largely useless for any sort of prediction. (It may be of interest that a cash prize offered for any evidence for the validity of popular astrology has never been claimed!)

The position, then, is that while there appears to be some mysterious connection between the movements of the planets and the personalities of people, this connection is, at least at present, of little value to selectors. Take, for example, Gauquelin's first great experiment. If research produced similar findings for 'outstanding managers' we would then know that people born under a particular planetary influence were a little more likely than others to be good managers. However, 80 per cent of 'outstanding managers' are born at the 'wrong' time — a revelation not helpful to the practising personnel executive!

There is, however, one way astrology can be used by personnel managers. Most candidates know their birth sign, many know what this signifies — and they often mention it. The interviewer can then say something like, 'I don't know anything about astrology; what are Scorpios (say) like?'. The candidate will then often say 'Well, Scorpios are bold, positive, decisive — sometimes impetuous — but I'm not like that ..'. This at least gives the interviewer some ideas of how the candidate sees him/herself.

Conclusion

While the techniques discussed in this chapter have their fascination and their historical interest they do not, at least as they stand at present, provide any simple, reliable way of understanding the personality of individuals or of predicting how they will behave in the future. In later chapters we will give consideration to other, perhaps more elaborate but more reliable, methods.

Further reading

Cheiro, *You and Your Hand*, Jarrolds, London, 1969. (Originally published 1933.)

Cooper, H. and Cooper P. *Heads*, London Phrenology Company, 1983.

Eysenck, H.J. and Nias, D.K.B. *Astrology: Science or Superstition?* Maurice Temple Smith, London, 1982.

Fowler, O.S. and Fowler, L.N. *Phrenology: A Practical Guide to Your Head*, Chelsea House Publishers, New York, 1969.

Gauquelin, M. *The Cosmic Clocks: From Astrology to Modern Science*, Paladies, St Albans, 1973.

Gauquelin, M. *Cosmic Influences on Human Behaviour*, Hodder & Stoughton, London, 1973.

Mackenzie Davey, D. and Harris, M. (eds), *Judging People*, McGraw-Hill, London, 1982.

Watson, L. *Supernature*, Hodder & Stoughton, London, 1973.

Chapter 2
Graphology

Graphology, the systematic study of handwriting, would appear to be a thoroughly justifiable enterprise. Handwriting is certainly highly individualistic: on receiving a letter from a friend, for example, there is rarely any need to open the envelope to find out who it is from. And, indeed, these personal handwriting styles appear very early. Even the writing of young children, being taught by the same teacher or using the same copy book, almost immediately shows marked individual differences. Some will be neat and tidy, some large, some small, some irregular, and so on. It is little wonder then that graphologists prefer the term 'brain writing' to handwriting. There does seem to be some mental intervention between the eye looking at the book and the reproduction of what has been seen on paper. And teachers will soon recognise the individual writing styles of their pupils. Handwriting, then, provides what has been called 'crystallised gestures' which are available to be measured in detail. There is, thus, a good *a priori* case for a scientific scrutiny of writing. And, indeed, graphologists have listed features for study. First it can be divided into three zones which can be studied separately: the Upper Zone (U/Z), the Middle Zone (M/Z) and the Lower Zone (L/Z). (see Figure 2.)

U/Z	Upper Zone		3	I
M/Z	Middle Zone		3	9mm
L/Z	Lower Zone		3	I

Figure 2 Graphology: zones of handwriting.

The following are some of the features graphologists believe merit careful study.

1. *Size*
   small
   average
   large

27

2. *Slant*
   left slant
   upright
   right slant
   changes in slant
3. *Width*
   narrow
   average
   broad
4. *Regularity*
   regular pattern
   average conformity
   irregular
5. *Letters connected or disconnected*
   all letters connected
   some letters connected, some disconnected
   all letters disconnected

There are further classifications of forms of connection and also the measurements such as pressure: thick, medium or thin line; falling downwards, remaining straight, or rising upwards; spacing between words; spacing between lines; margins (left, right, above and below and the various other combinations). Moreover, most of these characteristics can be analysed separately for each of the three zones U/Z, M/Z and L/Z!

Clear definitions, with examples, can be found in Jane Paterson's book *Interpreting Handwriting*.

Interpretation of writing features

As in palmistry (discussed in Chapter 1) most graphologists subscribe to the holistic approach and this provides a useful outlet for explaining why a particular feature does or does not predict a piece of behaviour or give evidence of a characteristic of personality. It can sensibly — albeit tiresomely for those interested in rigorous scientific analysis — suggest that any one feature may be highlighted, obscured or deflected by other features.

Consider just a few of the claims made for some of the major features in writing: the size of the writing.

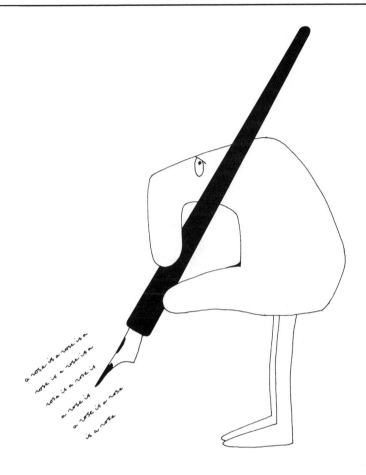

Small writing

It has been suggested that writers who keep their writing small are likely to be introverted, modest, humble and shunners of publicity. It is even suggested that the large writer may need a large house (and space for extravagant parties) whereas the small writer can be content with a small one. There is also the suggestion that, because we are in an age of specialisation in which increasing numbers of people have to concentrate on highly specialised jobs, there are now far more small writers. A century ago, it is argued, people were more active, more adventurous and that there were far more 'characters' about. These were conditioned to seek their fortune in the Empire.

Large writing

The large writer, it is suggested, shows a desire to 'think big' which, if supported by intelligence and drive, provides the ingredients for success. If the desire for largeness is turned inwards the individual may be vain and childishly keen on 'showing off'. (Most stars and celebrities it is said enlarge their writing: they enjoy fame and being in the public eye.) There is also a view that most world leaders have large writing. Yet the writing of Winston Churchill was not large and that of Mahatma Ghandi was small. (But then perhaps that reflected his style of leadership.) Similar generalisations are made about slant ('left slant writers are often found in jobs connected with history, the past or in research, backroom type jobs' — Jane Paterson).

Figure 3 Queen Elizabeth I's writing.

Upright writing

Upright writing is said to indicate self-reliance, poise, calm and self-collection, reserve, a neutral attitude, neither 'wholly for' nor 'wholly against'. The Queen and Prince Philip both have upright writing and so did Queen Elizabeth I (see Figure 3). Jane Paterson suggests that the extra large size and embellishments around her signature suggest the importance she had attached to her public image, which is mirrored in the magnificence of her dress.

I and ego

Graphologists have paid particular attention to how people write the personal pronoun 'I' (Figure 4). Here are some of the interpretations.

(i) A single writing stroke: 'I'. This is more often used by men and women educated at public schools. It has been said to reflect independence and self-confidence.

(ii) The form of 'I' which has a 'hat' and a 'pedestal': 'I'. This has a masculine bias and, it seems, is markedly prefered by left-handed people. Graphologists suggest that these people need a more personal emphasis on their ego.

There are various other forms (see Figure 4) but particularly interesting is the notably self-deprecating use of the lower case 'i'. Jane Paterson tells two interesting stories about different types of people who used this form. The first is from *Munby, Man of Two Worlds* by Derek Hudson.

Austin Dobson, the poet, wrote an effectionate tribute to his friend Arthur Munby, a Victorian barrister, poet, and civil servant. On Munby's death in 1910, Dobson said of his friend (who had 'pronounced opinions' on woman's rights and duties), that 'he has known many notables in art and letters and if his diaries should ever be published they could not fail to be interesting'. What he did not know was that Munby left three deed boxes to his old college, Trinity, Cambridge, with the proviso that they were not to be opened until 1950. On 14th January of that year, the Master of Trinity, GM Trevelyan, duly opened the boxes. In them were notebooks, manuscripts, sketch books and a complete run of Munby's personal diaries from 1858 to 1898, which were of great value.

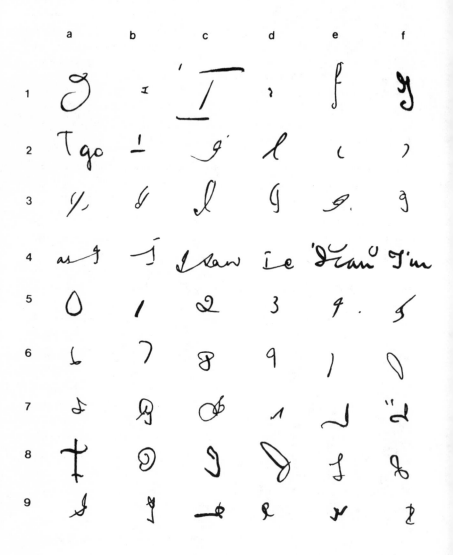

Figure 4 Fifty-four different personal pronoun 'I's, all taken from correspondence with the author. (Paterson, 1976)

Munby, it appeared, had a fascination for working women of all kinds and had secretly married at Clerkenwell Parish Church an attractive Shropshire maidservant named Hannah Cullwick. 'He had come to love her', said the will, 'with a pure and honourable love and not otherwise', but there had been one great snag; Hannah refused to become a 'lady'. She insisted on remaining Munby's servant, so he declared 'he had never been able to make known his marriage to his family'. Their life became very complex because of this; for example, his diaries say that when a clergyman friend called unexpectedly,

... making the best of the situation, I asked him to join me at dinner, and rang the bell. Instead of presenting our guest to my gentle graceful wife, and bidding him take the honour of a place by her at table, I had to treat her as one who served, and whom he would not care to notice.

The deed box opened by the Master of Trinity College also contained a number of letters from Hannah; one dated 14th September 1873, tells of her personal joy in looking after her superior husband. Throughout the letter she used the small form of the letter 'i' instead of the capital one:

... i made my mind up that it was best and safest to be a slave to a gentleman, nor wife and equal to any vulgar man.... i am as i am — a servant still, and a very low one.... i am united in heart and soul as well as married at Church to the truest, best and handsomest man in my eyes that ever was born....

The second story comes from Klara Roman's book, *Handwriting, A Key to Personality.* She writes about a young man who used this small form of the letter 'I' in his writing. He had run away from home at the age of thirteen and roamed about the country as a tramp. He worked as a handyman at a summer camp of artists. He was a talented but confused person, who regarded himself as worthless and useless; this self-devaluation was illustrated in his 'i'. One wonders whether someone noticing — perhaps a school teacher — when he began using this form of 'i', could not have built up his self-esteem and substantiated it before it was too late.

The validity of graphology

The efforts of psychologists to establish the validity (or otherwise) of such claims have yielded no positive results. Over the past fifty years many different approaches have been tried in particular in the relatively simple diagnosis of 'introversion/extraversion'. The overall conclusion appears to be that, in general, there is little relationship

A

The quick brown fox jumps over
the lazy dog.

B

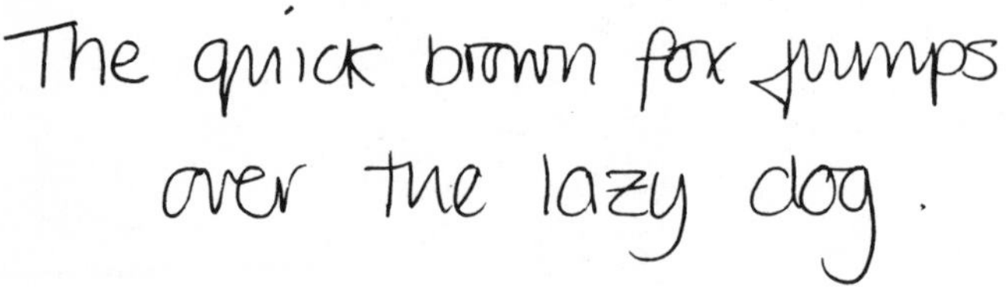

The quick brown fox jumps
over the lazy dog.

C

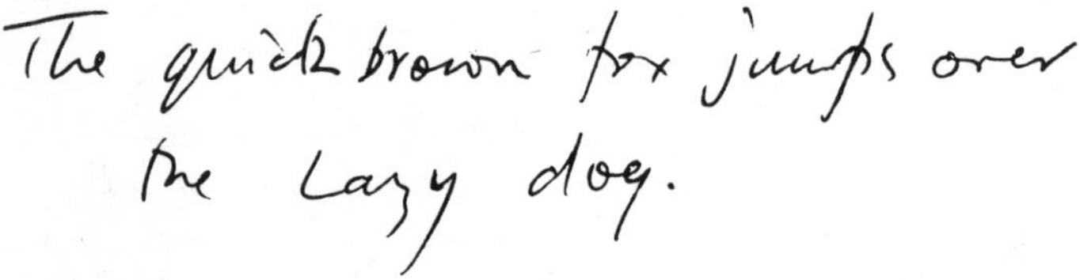

The quick brown fox jumps over
the Lazy dog.

D

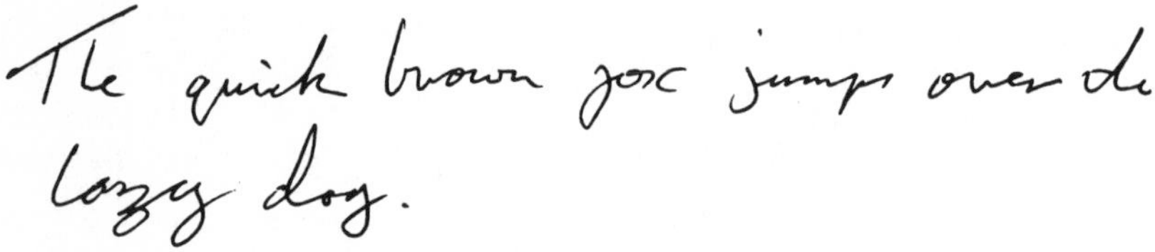

The quick brown fox jumps over the
lazy dog.

E

The quick brown fox jumps
over the lazy dog.

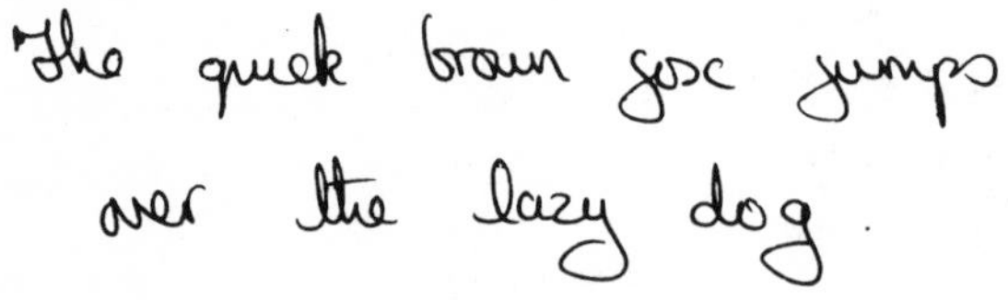

Figure 5 (A) and (B) are usually correctly identified as women's handwriting, (C) and (D) as men's. (E) is an example of 'sex-deviant' handwriting: though a woman's, it is usually identified as a man's. (Paterson, 1976)

between single graphic features and assessments of personality. These findings have not, however, convinced most graphologists or believers in graphology.

There is, however, one simple feature which may encourage hope. The sex of the author of a piece of handwriting can usually be told with above-average chance. In Figure 5 (A) and (B) are usually correctly identified as women's handwriting, (C) and (D) as men. (E) is an example of 'sex deviant' handwriting: though a woman's, it is usually identified as a man's.

Kate Loewenthal, who has done research in the field of handwriting and personality, accepts that handwriting is a good guide to sex (the main clue appears to be simple: circularity) but she adds 'it is hard to think of situations where this would be really useful'.

The holistic approach

With the introduction of computers it is now possible to conduct complex analyses with impressive speed. This has made it possible to see how combinations of handwriting features relate to personality. While there have been some positive results using this approach findings are, on the whole, disappointing. Yet there are some interesting by-products to this research. Judges will often have reasonably high levels of agreement about how neurotic or introverted the authors of handwriting are but these classifications do not generally agree with the personality test assessments of the writers.

In one study teachers and lecturers were asked to assess students' handwriting samples for traits which were important in academic assessment. There was good agreement on such traits as 'clear thinking', 'methodical' and 'original'. Whether these agreements were right or wrong it could, presumably, have some notable effect on the marking of examination papers. Certainly one study conducted by Markham found that essays in 'better' handwriting were given higher marks by teachers regardless of the content of the essays.

Signatures

Paterson has written interestingly on signatures. She points out that having a personal 'mark' has a long history and that it is important as a reflection of the inner self. She suggests that many people work at

devising signatures which will incorporate something from the signatures of people they admire. She also argues that while there is a constancy about the signature, a traumatic incident can bring about some changes. She reproduces Richard Nixon's signatures (Figure 6). Sceptics often offer a simpler explanation merely pointing out that someone who has to sign endless documents over many years may well streamline and simplify his signature.

Paterson's examples of signatures — and her comments on them — are of interest both in content and of evidence of the thinking of an imaginative graphologist.

Figure 6 The first signature of Richard Nixon in 1959. It appears to have plenty of vigour and drive, but notice how the exaggerated stroke of the 'x' is used to cross the name through. People often have premonitions of disaster and yet they are unable to quell or stifle the traits in their personality that drive them headlong towards it. In 1969 his signature shows severe shrinkage in the middle zone letters and the letter forms are blurred and illegible, showing that he is losing self-confidence and is uncertain of his image of the outside world. The third signature shows this process of shrinking becoming more marked, and the speed and drive more desperate. In the fourth signature the framework of the personality has gone; there is no strength, but more marked than ever is the crossing through of the void. (Paterson, 1976)

Elaborate symbolism in signatures can evolve through the influence of a profession or an overriding interest; the writer himself may be unaware of this. The signatures of two pilots are shown; one's signature is a design for a helicopter or whirly bird, the other underlines his very apt name with a paraph which is an exquisitely-drawn little jet plane.

The signature of Lord Hunt, famous for leading his successful expedition up Mount Everest. Is the flat at the start of his signature the one they photographed at the top of Everest? And is the end 't' cross, going up, symbolic of a rope flung upwards for further heights to climb?

Writing is frozen gesture. In the signatures of these famous dancers we can see graceful movements, heads held high, glides, leaps, pirouettes and patterns.

Another signature influenced by a profession? The writer is a sales director, selling cigarettes — perhaps a heavy smoker?

A signature connected with smoke or steam, which we can see curling away, is that of James Watt (left), inventor of the steam engine. On the right is the imaginative signature of an architect. Perhaps he designs high rise flats?

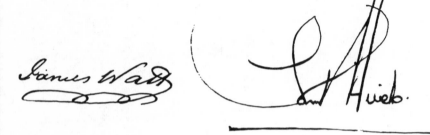

Another signature (left) that must take infinite trouble to execute. Compare it with the signature from the income tax inspector (right). He is certainly a faceless civil servant.

This is the signature of an official of the Henley rowing regatta. If you look at the signature from right to left, there is one stroke for the end of the boat, then eight oars, all rowing away. After this there are a few confused dots and dashes — staccato instructions coming from the cox to his crew? Then there is the cox at the extreme left, with his controls!

This is the signature of the late Sir Gerald Nabarro. His moustache features symbolically in the design, from wing tip to wing tip!

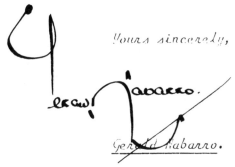

This is an unusual cypher or hall mark. It is totally illegible and without further enlightenment we can only guess that the writer's public image is dominated or obsessed by something which involves the number three. As the three strokes intersect his writing, he may well feel threatened by them. Could it be golf three times a week — or fishing likewise? Unlikely! He may be involved with some technical process — these could be bobbins or lines. He is the only one who can unlock the symbolism, although he may not be conscious of it when he is writing.

Here is another symbolic signature, but this time we know the answer — the signature belongs to George Best. Outlined in the unconscious symbolism is the structure of his problem. The design content is that despite only two possible L/Z movements, in the two G's of George, he produces four. The capital 'B' in 'Best' is extended into the L/Z, as is the end of the 't'. Two goals? Four posts? They are all crossed through by the line emphasizing his own name and underlining his signature. The story of his life?

The use of graphology in business

The use of graphology as a selection technique — or at least as part of the selection programme — has its attractions. It is relatively inexpensive, it does not involve the candidate in time-consuming group discussions or test sessions and it can be done covertly. There is plainly some ethical argument about the last point. Is it proper that an individual should be evaluated without his knowledge of this taking place? A copy of handwriting is not difficult to acquire and can be sent to the graphologist for a report without the candidate's knowledge. Indeed, job advertisements calling for application 'in the candidate's own handwriting' — far less frequent in the United Kingdom now than in the rest of Europe — are presumably not simply concerned with the neatness or the eligibility of the handwriting but the advertiser hopes to use this for either an amateur or professional judgement of the character of the candidate.

How widespread is the use of graphology in industry and commerce?

It is not easy to establish the number of organisations making use of graphology but at least one survey claimed that some 85 per cent of companies on the continent of Europe used graphology as at least part of their selection programme. In the United States of America the figure is far lower: 10 per cent of firms use graphology tests. The use in the United Kingdom is lower still: a recent IMS (Institute of Manpower Studies) survey found that some 5 per cent of employers used graphology as part of their selection procedure. And the even more recent Marplan survey indicated that 3 per cent of companies employing over 1000 employees used graphology.

In a private communication, Mr John Blomfield, Chairman of the British Institute of Graphologists writes,

... I did limited analyses of commercial clients serviced by our practising members, and extrapolating from that information we calculated that the total clientele numbered several thousand companies using graphology, in the main — but not solely — for personnel selection work.

He added,

Companies are generally unwilling to disclose their selection procedures, so I cannot give you names of those using graphology. There are, of course, a number of very good reasons why they should not disclose their hand, but it is a pity that we cannot support our case with some household names — and there are some!'

However, although there appears to be a good deal of scepticism in the United Kingdom, the use of graphology appears to be growing — 'by leaps and bounds' they say. Mr Blomfield did however produce some evidence by drawing attention to the fact that when he took over the chairmanship of the British Institute of Graphologists it had 180 members. Eighteen months later the membership was 245 and, added Mr Blomfield, 'every month sees new members joining'.

As Mr Blomfield pointed out, even those companies using graphology appear to be coy about the practice. We were able to get some 'household names' but when the personnel director (or whichever senior executive was responsible) was approached the response was generally something like, 'It may well be used in some of our outlying branches — we give our managers a great deal of autonomy — but it is not company policy'. Exceptions to this response according to a recent BBC *QED* programme were the bankers' Warburg and The Heron Company.

Other evidence of the difference of approach is reflected in entries in the *Yellow Pages*. In London, at the time of writing, there were 10 entries, whereas in Paris (with a far smaller population) there were 68.

A survey of the literature does little to encourage the scientific-minded investigator. Susan Taylor and Kathryn Sackeil in a paper published in May 1988 concluded

In the academic community where formal and rigorous validity tests are constructed, the use of graphology for employment decisions is viewed with considerable scepticism. Overall judgements often fail to predict relevant criteria such as performance evaluations.

Ben-Shakhar, Bar-Hillel and Bilu in two studies under the heading 'Can graphology predict occupational success?' concluded 'The graphologists did not perform significantly better than a chance model'.

One recent study is especially interesting because it was the joint effort of a psychologist (Rowan Bayne) and a graphologist and consultant (Francis O'Neill). They point out that not only is there a strong case for studying handwriting seriously as a method of personality assessment but, because it is widely used for selection and placement — especially on the continent of Europe — there is need for an incisive discussion on graphology's plausibility. Bayne, admitting to the weakness of much of the research carried out in the past, tried to design a 'fairly robust test of graphology'.

The method was to put together samples of handwriting from sixteen people — all students or ex-students of Bayne's. Two examples of handwriting were used, one from the subject's files (ie written before any knowledge of the study) and one written especially for the study on unlined paper. The judges were made up of:

- A trainee graphologist with less than a year's practical experience
- A professional graphologist with many years' experience, an authority in graphological circles, and the respected author of a major textbook on graphology
- Four graphologists who work as business consultants

The characteristics to be judged were from a contemporary psychological 'type theory' as measured by the Myers–Briggs type indicator (MBTI). The MBTI gives measures of extraversion/ introversion (E/I), sensing/intuition (S/N), thinking/feeling (T/F) and judging/perceptive (J/P). Graphologists were all familiar with this approach to personality and happy to be tested using it. Moreover, the descriptions from the test were judged to be accurate both by the 'subjects' and by Bayne.

The results of this study showed very clearly that none of the judges was able to judge the psychological types accurately, even though they were very confident of being able to do so both before and after making their judgements. Indeed, in one part of the experiment the group of four graphologists who chose (because of time) to assess only some of the samples, and taking any clear preferences as the criteria of accuracy, had the following results.

4 judgements of extraversion/introversion (E/I): 0 correct
6 judgements of sensing/intuition (S/N): 1 correct
4 judgements of thinking/feeling (T/F): 3 correct
6 judgements of judging/perceptive (J/P): 2 correct

Thus, out of 20 judgements, 6 were correct — less than the chance rate of 10!

While both Bayne and O'Neill were optimistic when they began the study they accepted the evidence of graphology's lack of validity at a formal level. Whereas Bayne is now more sceptical (and quotes, as one example, the three people who he *knows* — as surely as one can — as INFPs are confidently categorised by four expert graphologists as ESFJ, ESFJ, and ESFP,) O'Neill remains optimistic.

Conclusion

It is disappointing — and in many ways discouraging — that after almost a century and a half of formal study (graphologists gained academic recognition in Germany in the 1840s) the key to the interpretation of handwriting has not been found. Certainly it is not to be found in the crude measurements of such features as slant, size, pressure etc. In brief, a case has yet to be made for 'scientific' graphology. The fact that graphology is not a science does not, of course, preclude the existence of 'gifted' graphologists. There may be people who, perhaps without knowing quite how, can make remarkable judgements of personality and ability from specimens of handwriting; but there are also substantial numbers of charlatans in this field.

Perhaps the last words on this subject should be from Dr Loewenthal of the University of London:

People do agree quite well with each other about personality impressions conveyed by handwriting, but these impressions are not very accurate.... One should, therefore, be aware of one's own amateur attempts to read character from handwriting. Possibly the greatest danger is that these 'attempts' are largely unconscious. Professionally graphology may give better results, but it is not wholly reliable; there are probably cheaper and more valid methods of personality assessment to suit most contingencies.

Further reading

Courtis, J. *Interviews: Skills and Strategy*, Institute of Personnel Management, London, 1988.

Currer-Briggs, N., Kennett, B. and Paterson, J. *Handwriting Analysis in Business: The Use of Graphology in Personnel Selection*, Associated Business Programme, London, 1971.

Hargreaves, G. and Wilson, P. *A Dictionary of Graphology: The A–Z of Your Personality*, Peter Owen, London, 1983.

Mackenzie Davey, D. and Harris, M. (eds). *Judging People*, McGraw-Hill, London, 1982.

Nevo, B. (ed.). *Scientific Aspects of Graphology: A Handbook*, Charles C. Thomas, Springfield, IL, 1986.

Paterson, J. *Interpreting Handwriting*, Macmillan, London, 1976.

Chapter 3
Body Language

There is no doubt that there is a complex system whereby information and feelings are communicated through non-verbal channels involving gestures, body position, facial expressions and other devices. While much of the popular information is over-simplified — indeed, trivialised — it should be possible to approach this topic in a reasonably scientific and responsible way. However, neither this chapter nor, indeed, many of the larger texts, will provide any neat, straightforward guide to the interpretation of body language. If, however, it succeeds in persuading people to be more observant it should not only help them improve their skill in judging other people but also give them a sensitivity which can make them more attractive and more compassionate human beings. It may also help people to have an understanding of why they have certain intuitive reactions to others, some of which may advance their understanding — and some of which can distort it. For example, people may have considerably different views about their own territory — their own personal space. The size of this zone may be determined by crowding — people in big cities may tolerate a smaller zone than those in small towns or villages — and far smaller than those who live in the country. And there are almost certainly other cultural differences to be contended with. However, what appears to be undoubtedly true is that, should one person intrude on the personal space of another, this could be seen as a hostile act. Thus one can, quite unintentionally, generate hostility or be seen as 'pushy', or even as sexually aggressive, simply by standing closer to another person than the distance to which they are accustomed.

Space and status

In the business world, among the many symbols of status is the use of space. Senior managers will have larger offices and larger desks and so keep subordinates at a distance. Indeed, in some experiments it was possible to diagnose the status of a visitor to a high executive by his approach. Those with least status tended to stop when just inside the door and talk across the room to the seated man. Those with higher status walked half way up to the desk and those with most status went right up to the desk and stood directly in front of the manager.

Many senior managers, in addition to their desk and desk chairs also have a coffee-table arrangement in their offices. This allows the manager to indicate the type of interview which is likely to take place. If it is a reprimand to a subordinate, for example, it would almost certainly be a formal, across the desk, discussion; a visitor to be treated less formally and more warmly would be invited to sit in an easy-chair at the coffee table. What is involved is a matter of territory. The high status individual can invite the individual to share his territory or alternatively keep him at a distance.

It will not be possible in a chapter of this length to discuss anything like all the individual gestures and signals which can be generated with their possible interpretations. (Desmond Morris in *Manwatching* has classified various gestures and other 'behaviours' into 67 separate sections.) And, of course, all serious writers on body language discuss the importance of compound gestures — actions made up of a group of several distinct elements.

To give some idea of the complexity of interpreting body language let us consider the relatively straightforward area of deception. Consider, first, the actions which may accompany the telling of lies. Small children will often deliberately cover their mouth with one or both hands either while telling (or immediately after telling) an untruth. It is suggested that this gesture becomes modified and thus while a teenager will show more subtlety by moving fingers around the lips the adult may simply touch the upper lip or even the nose. However, while these gestures may be easily detected there can be many false-positives: the speaker may be perfectly truthful but have an itchy nose. Desmond Morris describes some of the work done by American researchers as follows:

They asked trainee nurses both to lie and to tell the truth about certain films they were shown. The young nurses were confronted with filmed scenes of gory operations such as limb amputation, and also with contrasting scenes of a harmless and pleasant nature. At a number of sessions, they were asked to describe what they saw, sometimes truthfully and at other times untruthfully. While they were doing this their every action and expression was recorded by concealed cameras. It was then possible to analyse in detail all the actions that accompanied truthful statements and all those accompanying deliberate lies, and to study the differences between them.

The nurses tried hard to conceal their lies because they were told that skill at deception was an important attribute for their future careers. This it is, for anxious patients require repeated reassurance that they are on the mend, or that risky operations are really quite safe, or that baffled doctors know exactly what their complaint is. What is more, they ask for this reassurance while at the same time being acutely tuned in for the slightest sign of any half-hidden pessimisms. To be a successful nurse one must learn to be a convincing liar. The experiment was therefore more than an academic exercise — and in fact it turned out that in later training the nurses who came top of their classes were also the ones who were the best body-liars in the film-report tests.

Even the best body-liars were not perfect, however, and the experimenters were able to assemble a set of key-differences in body actions between moments of truth-telling and moments of deception. They are as follows:

1. When lying, the nurses decreased the frequency of simple gesticulations they made with their hands. The hand actions they would normally use to emphasize verbal statements — to drive home a point, or to underline an important moment — were significantly reduced. The reason for this is that the hand actions, which act as 'illustrators' of spoken words, are not identified gestures. We know we 'wave our hands about' when we engage in excited conversation, but we have no ideas exactly what our hands are doing. Our awareness that our hands do something, but our unawareness of precisely what it is, makes us suspicious of the possible transparency of these actions. Unconsciously we sense that perhaps they will give us away and we will fail to notice, so we suppress them. This is not easy to do. We can hide them, sit on them, stuff them deep into our pockets (where they may still let us down by finding some coins and jingling them), or less drastically, we can clasp one firmly with the other and let them hold each other down. The experienced observer is not fooled by this — he knows that if those tiny hands are metaphorically frozen, there is something amiss.

2. When lying, the nurses increased the frequency of hand-to-face auto-contacts.

He goes on to point out that we all touch our faces from time to time during conversations but the number of times these simple actions are performed rises dramatically during moments of deception. These go well beyond the covering of the mouth mentioned above. Morris described the 'Chin Stroke', 'The Lips Press', 'The Nose Touch', 'The Cheek Rub', 'The Eyebrow Scratch', 'The Earlobe Pull' and 'The Hair Groom'. Going on to report the nurses behaviour he writes:

3. When lying, the nurses showed an increase in the number of body-shifts they made as they spoke. A child who squirms in his chair is obviously dying to escape and any parent recognises these symptoms of restlessness immediately. In adults they are reduced and suppressed — again because they are so obviously signs of unease — but they do not vanish. Watched closely, the adult liar can be seen to make tiny, vestigial body-shifts and to make them much more frequently than when telling the truth. They are no longer squirmings; instead they are only slight changes in the resting posture of the trunk as the speaker moves from one sitting posture to another.'

These unobtrusive body-shifts are saying: 'I wish I were somewhere else', the posture-changes being intensely inhibited intention movements of escape.

4. When lying, the nurses made greater use of one particular hand action, namely the 'Hand Shrug'. While other gesticulations decreased in frequency, this became more common. It is almost as if the hands were disclaiming any responsibility for the verbal statements being made.

5. When lying, the nurses displayed facial expressions that were almost indistinguishable from those given during truthful statements. Almost, but not quite, for there were, even in the most self-aware faces, tiny micro-expressions that leaked the truth. These micro-expressions are so small and so quick — a mere fraction of a second — that untrained observers were unable to detect them. However, after special training, using slow-motion films, they were able to spot them in normal-speed films of interviews. So, to a trained expert, even the face cannot lie.

These micro-expressions are caused by the face's all-too-rapid efficiency in registering inner feelings. When a mood-change seeks expression, it can expect to be registered by the alteration in the set of facial muscles in much less than a second. The counter-message from the brain, telling the face to 'shut up', often fails to catch up with the primary mood-change message. The result is that a facial expression begins and then, a split second later, is cancelled by the counter-message. What happens on the face during the split second delay is a tiny, fleeting hint of an expression. It is suppressed so quickly that most people never see it, but if watched for carefully during lying sessions, it can be detected and is then one of the best of deception clues.

Again, alas, it is not straightforward. For example, should an interviewer ask a candidate a difficult question he may well observe some chin stroking or brow scratching behaviour — not because the interviewee is about to lie but because he has to think out the answer to a complicated question.

Is it possible to tell lies successfully?

Certainly actors can learn to project an impression of relaxation when they may be tense and nervous. And there is no doubt that many confidence tricksters have a great deal of success. (And so, of course, do politicians, lawyers and many public figures.) Very often the give-away may not be in the relatively crude hand-to-face gestures but in other areas of the body. Most people know how their faces should appear when they are telling a particular story and they may know just how to present the words. They may not, however, be able to control other areas of the body quite as convincingly.

The eyes

> The eyes have one language everywhere.
>
> George Herbert, 1651

There is a wide belief that the eyes reveal a great deal about an individual. Such phrases as 'mean eyes', 'shifty eyes', 'beady little eyes', 'the evil eye', 'a gleam in the eye' and 'open-eyed' are all commonly used. Yet, perhaps there is more to be learned about the mood, feeling and reactions of people by observing the mouth than the eye. There is, however, one major eye signal which people find difficult to control — the dilation and constriction of the pupil. This is far more difficult to falsify than most other features: most people can adopt a happy, sad, aggressive, firm, pathetic face — and many others — but few can control the size of their pupils. The first major influence, of course, is the amount of light falling upon them. In a bright light they narrow to small black spots and in poor light they will expand to several times that size. They are also, however, affected by emotional factors. When we see something exciting or potentially pleasurable our pupils expand; similarly, when we see something unpleasant they contract. This is an area in which scientific analysis can be carried out. It is now possible, in laboratories, to show the degree to which people have been excited by pictures or other stimuli. (Great care is, of course, taken to ensure that the degree of light is stable and thus pupil dilations or constrictions are due to the impacts of the pictures shown.)

One early experiment involved showing photographs of human babies to men and women. These were divided into single adults (almost, by definition in those days, childless), the married but childless and the married with children. All women whether parents, married and childless or single, showed strong pupil dilation when shown these pictures. The single and married men without children, however, showed constriction, but the married men with children showed strong dilation. Thus it seems that until the human male actually has a baby of his own he does not respond with truly sympathetic emotion to other infants. (Perhaps proud parents should watch for the give-away hand-to-face signals when childless men 'coo' over their offspring!)

A favourite source of research has been sexual reactions to pictures of naked bodies and to pornographic films. Perhaps, predictably, findings have shown that pupils of homosexuals enlarge when they see the body of a member of their own sex and heterosexuals show similar responses to the opposite sex. An interesting aspect of these tests was that women, as well as men, found naked bodies more exciting than clothed ones. This contradicts the widely held view that women are not interested in 'pin-ups' or 'blue' films, at least not to the same degree as men.

These experiments have also been used to probe the genuineness of expressed attitudes. For example, a group of seemingly liberal-minded people, all of whom spoke approvingly of racial equality, were shown photographs of black males kissing white females. They divided into two very different groups: first the 'real' liberals whose pupils matched their beliefs and the 'psuedo' liberals who, in spite of their protests about equality, reacted negatively to the displays of black–white intimacy.

In another experiment an audience was shown two pictures of an attractive girl seemingly identical in all respects except that in one poster the pupils of the girl's eyes had been artificially enlarged. When asked to choose which girl they liked better, most men chose the one with the larger pupils without being able to explain why.

Experiments similar to those described above have also been used to provide some evidence that Don Juans — men who like to move briskly from one conquest to another — were more interested in girls whose pupils did *not* dilate in their presence. This perhaps suggests that they did not want to become associated with anyone who may become too involved.

It is also of interest that belladonna (literally 'beautiful woman'), the drug (atropine) prepared from the deadly nightshade — the poisonous plant *Atropa belladonna* — has been used over the ages to enlarge the pupils of women who wished to attract men.

It is also reported that Chinese gem dealers used to observe the pupils of possible buyers in order to judge their reactions to a particular item and so give them guidance on where to pitch the price.

Gaze in person perception

Various studies have been carried out to assess the importance of eye contact in employment interview evaluation. Mark Cook describes an experiment in which photographs were taken of candidates first looking straight into the camara and secondly looking downwards. Forty-four job interviewers in an employment agency were assigned one of the photographs. Each subject was told to assume that he or she was interviewing a person for the job as a management trainee. The results showed that interviewees were more likely to be hired if they looked straight ahead rather than down. In addition, those who looked straight ahead were rated as being more alert, assertive, dependable, confident, responsible and having more initiative.

In Young and Beier's experiment, in which a number of interviewees were video-taped using different non-verbal behaviours in a short job interview with a standard content, applicants who had greater amount of eye contact, more head movements, and who smiled more, were rated higher on job acceptability.

Pease describes a number of types of 'gaze behaviour'. He discusses that while some can make people feel comfortable, others can make them feel ill-at-ease and some can even carry suggestions of untrustworthiness. This, he claims, is primarily to do with the length of time they look at the other person. He refers to Argyle's hypothesis that if person A likes person B he will look at him a lot. This causes B to think A likes him, so B will like A in return. In other words, to build a good rapport with another person the gaze should be held for about 60–70 per cent of the time. But Pease goes further, pointing out that not only is length of gaze significant — just as important is the area of the person's face and body which is the object of the gaze. He discusses the following styles for different situations.

The business gaze. In business discussions it is suggested that the gaze should be directed around a triangle on the other person's forehead. This, it is suggested, creates a serious atmosphere and the other person senses you mean business. Only if the gaze drops below the level of the other person's eyes could control of interaction be lost.

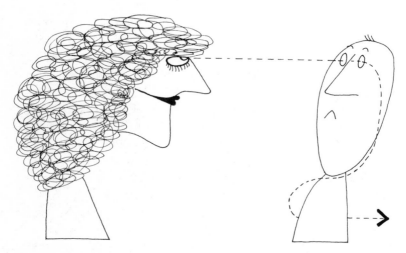

The intimate gaze. This gaze is across the eyes and below the chin to the other person's body. Both men and women are said to use this gaze to show interest in each other and those who are interested will return the gaze.

Sideways glance. This, it is suggested, is used to create either interest or hostility. When combined with a slightly raised eyebrow or a smile it communicates interest and is frequently used as a courtship signal.

Combined with down-turned eyebrows, furrowed brow or the corners of the mouth down turned, it signals a suspicious, hostile or critical attitude.

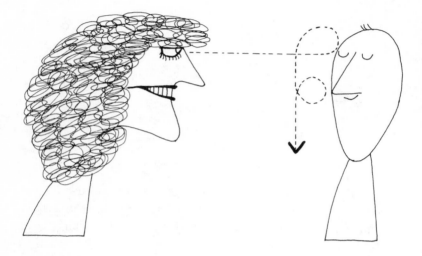

Countering gaze ploys

It is possible to block the attempts to be influenced by the various gaze techniques discussed above. One method is to close the eyes for a second or two thus shutting out the influence.

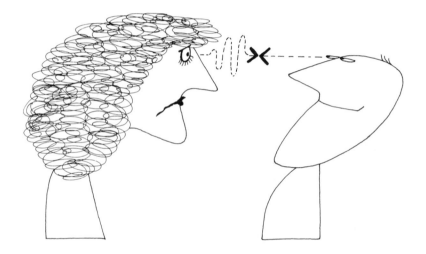

More positively there is the gesture of tilting the head backwards giving a long look, perhaps with half-closed eyes, which has given rise to such popular expressions as 'look down upon' and 'looking down one's nose at'.

Posture and gesture in courtship

Men and women transmit signals to each other some of which are conscious and deliberate while others almost wholly unconscious.

Preening behaviour

In males this may involve tie straightening, hair smoothing and the adjustment of cuffs. This may be followed by more open sexual display such as the thrusting forward of the pelvis and adopting a fingers in the belt 'prowling posture'. Men may also, when in groups, be seemingly truculent, aggressive or insulting. This is presumably designed to prompt a response which will lead to closer contact.

Women appear not only to be far more subtle in their approaches but also to have a far greater range of signals. There is a similar preening behaviour including the apparent adjusting of the hair which also has the effect of drawing attention to the breasts.

The use of palms and wrists

Pease suggests that an interested female will expose the skin of her wrists to a potential male partner.

More obvious, legs are often open wider than would have been the case had the male not been present. This contrasts with the behaviour of the sexually defensive woman who keeps her legs crossed and together at all times.

When the first stage — the eye-to-body one — has been passed, the next is the eye-to-eye contact. This may often begin with a quick glance, usually reinforced by smiling and more than usual moistening of the lips. At such times the eyes are wide open and there is likely to be the pupil dilation as discussed earlier.

Next is talking — this, in some social groups, can move from the exchange of insults to an exchange of information — a process of learning about each other. A significantly important stage in courtship is touching. Should this be misjudged it can, as with the invasion of personal territory, appear threatening and hostile. Very often the first touch is a disguised act of support, or giving guidance — such as taking an arm to help the partner across the street, helping with coats, or the carrying of packages.

The process can then be advanced by such activities as dancing. If the signals remain positive this is likely to move on to further body contact, arm-to-waist, mouth-to-hand (or now more likely to face) leading to mouth-to-mouth kissing.

Of course, just as there are 'come hither' gestures there are blocking signals — folded arms, for example, can present a barrier with a clear message of 'keep off'.

In many situations it will not be quite as clear and there will be partial barriers.

Conclusion

There seems every reason to believe that some study of body language can sharpen one's appreciation of these non-verbal communications and help one to make sounder judgements of others. It can also introduce a fascinating hobby: as Desmond Morris says:

Just as a bird watcher watches birds, so a man watcher watches people. But he is a student of human behaviour, not a voyeur. To him, the way an elderly gentleman waves to a friend is quite as exciting as the way a young girl crosses her legs. He is a field observer of human actions, and his field is everywhere — at the bus stop, the supermarket, the airport, the street corner, the dinner party and the football match. Wherever people behave, there the man watcher has something to learn — something about his fellow men and, ultimately, about himself.

Body language and personnel selection

While there seems little doubt that greater attention to body language will give a deeper understanding of attitudes and relationships, relatively few people would claim it to be sufficient in itself to be a selection method. It seems likely, however, as with many other techniques, there may be gifted practitioners.

If, as some would claim, it can provide accurate information on the ability and personality of the individual then, like handwriting, it can be used covertly. There was, for an example, an executive search consultant who cooperated with a body-language expert. Their arrangement was that the 'headhunter' would lunch with the candidate on a particular day in a particular restaurant and the body-language consultant would arrange to have a table nearby. He would then observe the candidate and record his observations. (An elaborate recording system exists.) Thereafter he would interpret his notes and present a report describing the personality and ability of the candidate. The candidate would remain unaware of this having happened. Again, as with graphology, some would argue that this was an unethical approach and that the candidate should be made aware that he was being assessed, not only on his luncheon conversation but by a trained observer. Most practitioners in body language — and there are not many — make their observations in a conventional interview and this makes research into the validity difficult. It is almost impossible to know to what degree the judgements of body movement were influenced by the content of the interview and by other 'intuitive reactions' to the person concerned. Indeed, it has been argued that successful body-language consultants are gifted judges who could equally well be using tea-leaves or head bumps. Such a charge would appear to be unfair: as indicated in this chapter, there is ample evidence that physical and physiological changes do reflect underlying attitudes and so can be used to help to predict future behaviour.

In summary, it appears plain that anyone concerned with judging people would be careless, indeed, profligate, to discard the evidence of body language. It should, however, usually be used in conjunction with other methods such as the interview and psychological testing. It is a valuable aid rather than a method to be used in isolation.

Further reading

Ardrey, R. *The Territorial Imperative*, Collins, London, 1967.
Argyle, M. *Bodily Communication*, Methuen, London, 1975.
Courtis, J. *Interviews: Skills and Strategy*, IPM, London, 1988.
Fast, J. *Body Language*, Pan, London, 1971.
Lamb, W. *Body Code — The Meaning in Movement*, Routledge & Kegan Paul, London, 1979.
Lamb, W. *Posture and Gesture*, Duckworth, London, 1965.
Morris, D. *Man Watching: A Field Guide to Human Behaviour*, Cape, London, 1977.
Pease, A. *Body Language*, Sheldon Press, London, 1984.
Wainwright, G. R. *Body Language*, Teach Yourself Books, Hodder & Stoughton, Sevenoaks, 1985.

Chapter 4
The Interview

Almost thirty years ago, Professor Eysenck wrote: 'We must conclude that the interview is almost a complete failure and the time devoted to it as far as accuracy of prediction is concerned goes wasted'. Recent studies (such as IMS Report No 160 by Bevan and Foggatt) tend to support this view and so provide little comfort for those using this most widely used of selection tools. There is, however, some evidence that trained interviewers are better than untrained interviewers.

This chapter offers the interviewer some advice on how best to conduct the 'non-directive' interview and how to prepare for a 'structured' or 'behaviour description' interview. As the employment interview is perhaps, out of all the different types of interview, the one most concerned with judging people, this has been selected as a model for this chapter.

Why the interview?

The selection interviewer should have three main aims:

1. Collecting information about candidates so that certain judgements can be made about them.
2. Giving information: in the employment interview the candidate needs information about the company, the job, the conditions and the prospects, etc.
3. Beginning the induction process. The interview, if not the first impression gained by the candidate, will almost certainly be one of the most powerful early impressions. How interviews are conducted will influence the employee's attitude towards the organisation very strongly.

Before the interview

Try to make sure that the candidate's first impressions are favourable. The attitude of the receptionist or the security man can be vital. Evidence that the candidate is expected and known by name makes a favourable first impression.

The waiting time should be minimal and as comfortable as possible for the candidate.

The interview room

The person to be interviewed should feel as relaxed and comfortable as possible so make sure that there is a comfortable chair available, that you will not be interrupted by telephone or by people coming in, and that you can see the time without having to look at your watch.

The atmosphere will probably be more informal if you do not sit behind a desk. Many people find the coffee-table arrangement an agreeable one.

Preparing yourself and making a checklist

At the end of the non-directive interview you will want to make a number of judgements about the candidate and there will be a number of questions which you will want to be able to answer. For instance:

- Is he intelligent enough to do the job? (or too intelligent for it?)
- Is he likely to stay (or is he too ambitious, or foot-loose?)
- How will she respond to the type of supervision she will have?
- How will she get on with her fellows?
- Will her family responsibilities make it possible for her to do overtime?
- Will he be a reliable worker? (does he stick at things or give up easily?)
- How does he stand up to pressure?
- Is he wanting the job only for the money?

To answer questions of this kind you will want as much information as you can get about a person's life history: very often your best evidence for how someone is going to behave in the future is how he has behaved in the past. In addition you will want to know about his present circumstances.

What follows is for the non-directive interview. Preparation for the structured or 'behaviour description' interview is discussed later in the chapter — as is planning for the panel (or board) interview.

68

Making your checklist

Read any job description or 'person specification' that has been provided, and make a note of any points arising from them on which you particularly want to get evidence.

Read any application form carefully and note any gaps in the recorded history that you want to have filled in, or anything unusual that you want to learn about in more detail. In case the candidate does not volunteer such information, add to the list a reminder to prompt him to tell you about:

- spare-time activities
- domestic circumstances and responsibilities
- health record
- ambitions
- reasons for leaving previous jobs
- best and worst subjects at school (in some cases this can be a pointer to a person's level of intelligence).

Alec Rodger's Seven Point Plan (Table 2) provides a further checklist.

Conducting the interview

What kind of interview?

The following exchange is typical of many interviews conducted by well-meaning people.

INTERVIEWER: I see from your application form that you went to Brinkley School and got four 'O' levels, and then you went to the local Tech and got your HNC, and then you got a job with the Alpha Company as a trainee technician in their laboratories. And you stayed there two years, and then you moved to the Beta group where you worked in the quality control department.

APPLICANT: Yes, that's right.

That didn't tell anyone anything; and what's more it was a waste of valuable interviewing time.

Table 2 The Seven Point Plan

1. Physical make-up

   Has he any defects of health or physique that may be of occupational importance? How agreeable are his appearance, his bearing and his speech?

2. Attainments

   What type of education has he had? How well has he done educationally? What occupational training and experience has he had already? How well has he done occupationally?

3. General intelligence

   How much general intelligence can he display? How much general intelligence does he ordinarily display?

4. Special aptitudes

   Has he any marked mechanical aptitude? manual dexterity? facility in the use of words? or figures? talent for drawing? or music?

5. Interests

   To what extent are his interests intellectual? practical-constructional? physically-active? social? artistic?

6. Disposition

   How acceptable does he make himself to other people? Does he influence others? Is he steady and dependable? Is he self-reliant?

7. Circumstances

   What are his domestic circumstances? What do the other members of the family do for a living? Are there any special openings available for him?

During the part of the non-directive interview when you are getting information about a candidate, your job is essentially to listen. It is not to talk, not to read the candidate's application form to him, not to ask a stream of questions.

Obviously you will have to ask some questions, but if you can get the candidate to give you a more-or-less biographical account of his life you will find that you need to ask relatively few. And if you get him to do this in a relaxed way, he will tell you a lot more than the bare facts.

How to open the interview

Unfortunately, the candidate will usually come along expecting to be asked a lot of questions. So when you first meet him, discuss the weather or his train journey (or any other ice-breaker) for a moment or two, and then explain what kind of interview it is going to be, and the order of events. You might say, *'First I will try to tell you anything you want to know about the job, and then I'll ask you to tell me about yourself — it's not going to be a formal interview with me asking a lot of questions'.*

After you have answered his questions, you might point to his application form, or wave it gently at him and say something like: *'This has given me the outline of your history, and now I'd like you to fill it out. Can you tell me about how you came to take these various jobs, and how you liked them, and so on. In fact I would find it helpful if you could start at the beginning and tell me something about your early days — your family and where you lived — and then go on to your schooling and the jobs you have had up to date, and anything else that has happened to you.'*

You must, however, be flexible. Sometimes the candidate will want to tell you about his qualifications, or what he does in his present job, as soon as he has heard your account of the job that he is applying for. Don't stop him short or you will start the interview on the wrong note. Let him talk about what is uppermost in his mind and then ask him to go back to the beginning so that you will have the complete picture.

How to get the candidate to talk: dos and don'ts

During the interview you want to encourage the candidate to keep talking about himself. You may want to get him to go back and enlarge on some points that he dealt with only very briefly when he was recounting his history, or you may want him to fill in gaps.

Here are some tips — some 'dos' and 'don'ts' of interviewing.

Do say 'Tell me about . . .' This is one of the most valuable phrases you can use. It is valuable because it is neutral: it gives no indication to the candidate of what sort of answer will win your approval. It is also valuable because it invites more than just 'Yes' or 'No'. But using it takes a little practice, and the next 'Do' point is important.

Do pause. If you use wide, open-ended questions such as, *'Tell me about...'* or *'Can you tell me more about...'* then you must give the candidate time to gather his thoughts and decide how he is going to present them.

An inexperienced interviewer often finds silence intolerable. He makes a good start by asking an open-ended question, but when the person does not answer instantly he bursts in with another. For example, a question like, *'Can you tell me some more about your education?'*, leaves the candidate wondering whether he should start by telling you about his recent evening course or about what he did at his secondary school or he should start right at the beginning with his small village school. These reflections clearly take time, and it is here that the interviewer who cannot stand the suspense comes in with a question such as *'Well, did you pass the eleven plus?'*. This of course gives relief to the candidate: he can sit back and answer questions and leave all the thinking to the interviewer.

You should try to make it clear to the candidate, courteously and gently, that he is the person who is expected to do the talking. You do not use the pause to place the man under stress, but simply to encourage him/her to talk about him/herself. (Once they get started, most people enjoy this; they are talking about a subject in which they are very interested, after all. The great majority can be persuaded to talk easily and openly about themselves.)

Do repeat short replies with '?' Even when you use the 'tell me about' type of question you may sometimes get a laconic answer. Should this happen, first try the pause to indicate that you expect that the candidate will expand the brief reply. If this does not work, try repeating the answer back to the candidate, but in a tone of voice which adds a question mark to it. For example:

INTERVIEWER: Can you tell me about what you do in your spare time?
CANDIDATE: Hospital visiting. [*pause*]
INTERVIEWER: Hospital visiting?

At this stage it is possible that the person may say '*Yes, hospital visiting*', but it is unlikely. It is much more probable that she will go on to explain how often she does this, and what led her to start doing it, and quite possibly her views on the problems of old people as well.

As a last resort you can say '*I'd be interested to hear more about that*', but try the other techniques first: they can help to encourage the candidate to talk freely.

Do show interest. Your facial expression can do a great deal to encourage (or discourage) the candidate. If you acknowledge what he says with a smile and a nod of interest he is more likely to continue doing it than if you appear to be ignoring what he says, or to be bored by it. (By showing your interest you are, in effect, 'conditioning' the candidate to continue talking.)

There is a particular danger that the serious interviewer may not make it plain that he is interested. In attending to what the candidate is saying he is likely to be thinking hard; and when people think hard they often frown or even adopt an expression which looks like a scowl. If an interviewer does this, the candidate is likely to stop talking.

If you consistently use the 'tell me about' approach, you should not need the advice given in the following list of 'Don'ts'. But read it anyway; even experienced interviewers can fall into bad habits without being aware of them.

Don't ask 'yes/no' questions. If you ask a question which allows the simple answer 'Yes' or 'No', that is what you will often get. In reply to *'Did you spend any of your holidays abroad?'* the candidate may well say *'No'*. So the ball is back with you and you have got to ask another question and you've got the beginning of an interrogation going.

By the same token, avoid asking any questions which can be answered very briefly. *'How is your health?'* is likely to produce the short reply *'Good'*. *'Could you tell me about your health record?'* can be much more fruitful.

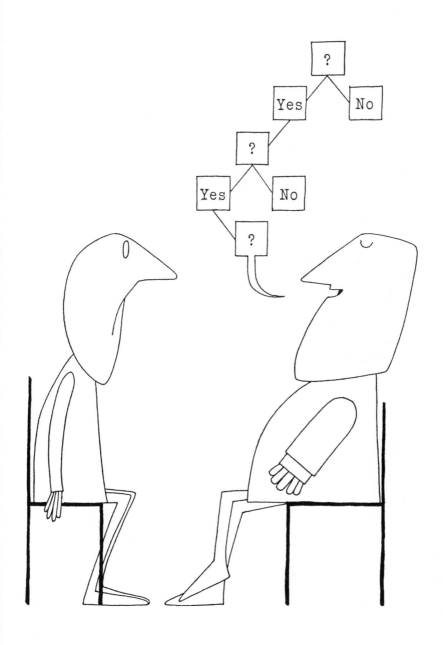

Don't ask leading questions. Avoid asking questions which indicate the answer you expect. '*I imagine you would like to attend a course in computer programing?*' or '*I expect you are pretty good at filing*', makes it fairly clear to the candidate how he should reply.

Here is a less direct form of leading question: '*Now we are in an industry with a rapidly expanding technology, so it is important that our people keep up to date. Also I should warn you that it is a tough job, not the sort of thing that can be done on a 9 to 5 basis — although it is a growing organisation and there is plenty of opportunity for promotion. Now tell me how you think you might shape up to what we want.*' To this the shrewd candidate might say something like: '*Well, I think you ought to know that I am very ambitious and it is vital to me that the job I take has good prospects. And in order to get on I don't mind a bit the number of hours I put in. Oh, and I should mention that I am something of the permanent student so that if there are some evening classes available I would be keen to go.*' Whereupon, the naive interviewer might say, '*Marvellous, just the man we are looking for.*'

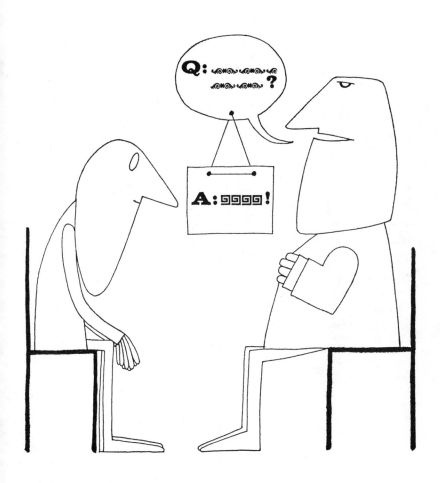

Don't criticise. Remember that you want to keep him telling you about himself; if you show disapproval of what he says, you are liable to stop him short. Here is a classic example from a practice interview:

CANDIDATE: ... so I dropped French at that stage.
INTERVIEWER: Well, that was very silly of you.

After this experience, every single piece of information had to be dragged from the reluctant subject.

Don't bring him back to the point too abruptly. When you ask the 'tell me about' type of questions, the candidate may drift from the main point; and you may be tempted to correct this. In many situations it will be more profitable to let him continue — you may well learn something important, and you can encourage him later to go back to the original point.

In reply to *'Tell me about your last job'* the candidate might say, *'Well, I started in the packing department but then my husband went on to night shift and he wasn't able to sleep properly in the daytime and he was getting a lot of headaches. I made him go to to the doctor in the end and he had to go into hospital for an examination and it turned out he had this nerve disease, so now he can only work part time and doesn't bring in much money. So I had to look for another job that paid better.'*

When she started to talk about her husband, the interviewer might have cut her off: *'No, no, I don't want to hear about your husband at this stage, I want to hear about you last job.'* If this had happened the facts about her husband's illness and its effect on the family finances might not have emerged later.

Don't raise personal matters too soon. There are times when it is important to know in some detail about certain aspects of a candidate's private life. But it would be an obvious mistake to pick up the application form at the beginning of the interview, refer to the fact that the candidate has said that she is divorced, and ask her to expand on this. (It has been known to happen.) Not the first question. Later, when rapport has been established, the information is likely to come out easily and naturally.

Don't ask gimmicky questions. Some interviewers have 'pet' questions which sound searching and deep, but which do not yield any information which can be sensibly interpreted. Interviewers pose riddles, for example, or problems with a catch in them without having any clear reason for doing so. The most likely effect is to bemuse the candidate or even humiliate him.

How to control the very talkative candidate

From time to time you may find yourself interviewing an exceedingly talkative candidate — the man who, with a third of the allotted interview time gone, is still telling you about his very early childhood. What do you do?

There is no straightforward answer, and you have to use your judgement in the circumstances. But you will have to interrupt — though not in the middle of a sentence. Wait for a suitable moment and then you might say: *'Thank you, that was interesting; I wonder if you could now just give me a summary of what happened after that — I'd like to get the overall picture first and then we can come back to particular points.'* Other useful phrases include, *'Fine, so that brings us up to date; can I now ask you to tell me...'* or *'Good, could we not turn to ...'* or, in extreme cases, *'Can I now ask you to jump ahead to ...'.*

You will, however, often be able to spot the garrulous candidate very early in the interview: he will make it clear in the first few minutes that he is likely to talk at very great length. When someone does this you would be wise to ask him to give you a brief account of his background (you need not fear that it will be too brief).

How to round off and close the interview

Consult your checklist. Before you let the candidate go, make sure that there are no major gaps in the information that you have got. There is no reason why you should not consult any list of points that you made before the interview. Do this openly, explaining to the candidate what you are doing. You can then say, '*Oh, yes, there was one point I wanted to ask you to tell me about....*'.

Invite the candidate to add or modify. Ask him to tell you anything about himself that has not come up in the main part of the interview and which he thinks may be important (and invite him to raise any more questions that have occurred to him). But allow him time to think about this; indeed, suggest that he may want a few moments to do so.

Also, you would be wise to invite him to expand on any of the things he has said which he thinks you may have misunderstood.

Extend the interview on the way out. Arrange to show the candidate out yourself whenever possible; you may collect useful extra information in the course of chatting to him on the way. When the interview has officially ended and any slight tension has relaxed, he may well tell you new facts about himself as you are seeing him to the door.

Tell him when he will hear from you. Be as honest as possible in explaining when he can expect to hear from the company again. If it is the case that you have more people to see, tell him so. If there is a possibility that he may be asked to come back to meet someone else, tell him so. And, as a last word, you might ask him whether he is now seriously interested in the job.

Making judgements about the candidate

This section deals with a number of general points about which you may be required to make a judgement. Remember, very often your best evidence of how someone is likely to behave in the future is how he has behaved in the past. You should not attach a great deal of importance to a single incident but be on the lookout for recurring or consistent themes in his background.

First impressions

These are of primary importance in jobs such as sales, reception, public relations, etc. Do not rely simply on your own first impression but ask other people who have had contact with the candidate for their initial reaction.

Level of intelligence (see Chapter 5)

First, some warnings. Don't confuse level of intelligence with level of education; a first-class degree in mathematics is clear evidence of a great deal of brain power, but the fact that someone does not have any formal educational qualifications does not necessarily mean that he is lacking in this. (He may not have passed examinations because he was applying himself hard to other interests when he was at school or college.) And don't assume that for all jobs the higher the intelligence the better. There are many jobs which do not require a lot of intelligence; and a very clever person in an undemanding job is likely to become frustrated.

Don't think that you can judge level of intelligence from someone's appearance; this is a well-known trap. It has been demonstrated, for example, that people who wear glasses are likely to be rated by untrained observers as more intelligent than those who do not!

In the absence of an intelligence test — the best way of assessing intelligence (see Chapter 5) — you should consider closely such matters as the person's education and career record, outside interests, etc. Is there evidence, for instance, that he studied hard at school but nevertheless was consistently unsuccessful at examinations? The following are also pertinent:

- What were his best subjects? (facility at mathematics and physics is generally a positive sign).
- Has he ever shown a genuine interest in 'intellectual' pastimes (playing chess, doing complex crossword puzzles)?
- What sort of things does he read, or used he to read?
- How did he get on at any selection boards for the services or other bodies?
- Has he ever been offered a job by a company known to use intelligence tests as part of their selection procedure?
- In the interview does he appear quick to take points?
- What sort of questions does he ask?

Verbal skill

Here your main evidence is likely to be how he 'comes across' in the interview. Assuming that you have been able to get him to relax and do some talking, is he:

- fluent?
- does he speak clearly?
- can he give an account of something without losing the point?
- does he use words (and grammar) correctly?
- is his manner of speaking lively or dull?

Note: If the job calls for someone who can express himself in a clear, orderly way on paper, don't take his word for it that he is good at this. And remember that someone may have helped him to write his letter of application. If you can, devise a way to get him to write something while he is on your premises.

Motivation/ambition

What does he say he is aiming at, and does this appear realistic? (He could be trying to 'prove' something, to 'keep up' with his father or brothers — what are their occupations? If he is aiming too high he might become frustrated or discontented rather quickly.)

- Is he so absorbed in his spare-time interests that he is likely to be distracted from his work?
- Does his history provide evidence that he is prepared to give up leisure activities, see less of his family, tolerate unpleasant conditions in order to get ahead?
- Do his domestic commitments (mortgages, etc) suggest that his need to earn a certain amount of money will dominate all else?

Is he likely to stay?

Again a good area for examining how he has behaved in the past. Has he been a job hopper? Learn about his family and domestic circumstances: does he or she have to be tied to one place? Or is there a primary concern to earn money? Career aims may be important — will there be appropriate prospects for the candidate in your company?

Energy and perseverance

Once again you may get evidence from educational history, job history, perhaps from spare-time activities.

- Did he plug away until he passed those exams, even though he had some early failures?
- Has he gained qualifications by correspondence or night classes?
- Has he often started training courses, or taken up hobbies, and then abandoned them?
- Does he pursue his outside interests with great intensity? (A note of warning here: he may not transfer his energy on the football field to the work situation.)
- Is there anything in his job history which suggests that he likes to see things through?

Initiative and independence

Of vital importance here is, in all but the youngest of candidates, past history. Has he made his own way or been led by others?

Emotional maturity and the ability to tolerate stress

Even if it is very well conducted the interview can represent a minor stress situation and provide some information about a candidate's emotional control. 'Nervous' habits — tics, twitching, excessive fiddling — may be evident, for example.

- In talking about himself, is he prepared to admit that he can make mistakes? (Or have his misfortunes, according to him, always been someone else's fault?)
- Do his references to other people suggest that he has not come to terms with the fact that he was unlucky, or deprived, when he was young?
- Does his account of past happenings suggest that he has suffered disappointments, or experienced 'tough' situations, without being too upset?
- Does he appear to have a stable domestic life? (This is a sensitive area about which you may get little or no evidence; and you should be careful not to over-interpret any evidence you do get.) Similarly with his health record: you should be aware that asthma, migraine, ulcers, 'stomach upsets', insomnia can be 'nervous' symptoms, but that they may be important only if the candidate reports that they always occur, in a rather extreme form, when he is under pressure.

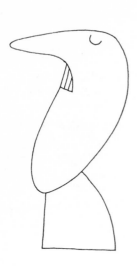

Relationships with other people

- Does he give credit to others, for example, or is his account of himself strongly self-centred?
- Is he consistently critical of the people he has worked with in the past?
- Does he appear to be strongly status-conscious?
- Has he been a 'participator' in the past? Or are his interests and hobbies entirely solitary?

A last word to the interviewer

The style of interviewing recommended here takes a good deal of self-discipline: to sit back and listen may sound easy but it often needs a conscious effort not to interrupt and to suspend one's judgement until there is evidence available.

It is also of vital importance for the interviewer to be aware of his own prejudices. Was he over-impressed by social and educational background, or prejudiced by a limp handshake or suede shoes? The more you can learn about yourself, the better you will be as an interviewer.

The structured interview

This chapter so far has been essentially concerned with the unstructured or non-directive interview. It has been subjected to severe criticism (see p. 67). One suggested way of improving this seemingly haphazard technique is to give it structure. The advocates of this technique point out that using standard sets of questions means that each applicant will be taken over the same ground and thus the judgements will be fairer. This approach is far from new: Sir Cyril Burt produced a schedule in the 1920s. Wonderlic (an American designer and user of intelligence tests) and McMurry (another distinguished psychologist) gave support for patterned interviews. Perhaps the best known scheme in the United Kingdom is the one produced by Professor Alec Rodger — The Seven Point Plan (see Table 2, p. 70). Rodger, however, did not suggest the plan be used as a series of questions but rather as a checklist to ensure that all the relevant ground was covered and as a way of classifying the information. He did not, for example, suggest that the information be collected in the order laid down by the plan but drew the analogy with the sorter in a post office classifying the information under the various headings as he received it.

Rodger also emphasised that the questions under the seven headings were not meant to be put directly to the applicant but that they were questions for the interviewer to ask himself about the applicant at the end of the interview. It provides a checklist to enable the interviewer to say 'What shall I ask about next?'. Thus the Seven Point Plan can be used by the 'unstructured' interviewer as well as a basis for a structured interview.

The research into the structured interview moved from considering the set of 'all purpose' questions for all jobs to the study of specific job requirements and a design of questions to elicit the appropriate information. And, indeed, in any interview there is a strong argument to support the view that knowledge of particular job requirements enhances interview judgements.

An interesting side-line on the research in this field provided some evidence that interviewers who took notes during the interview had the highest retention for information thus providing evidence to support taking notes *during* the interview as well as making notes *before* assessing the candidate.

Job analysis

Job analysis is the systematic examination of a job in detail to identify its component tasks. Job analyses may be undertaken for a number of purposes such as job evaluation (to establish a fair payment system) for establishing training needs, for manpower planning, etc. In this section we will be concerned with its use for designing an interview of a type which many people believe to be an effective way of judging a person's suitability for a particular job. Much of the best work is based on the 'critical incident technique' — a method introduced in the 1950s by John Flanagan. His work derived from reviewing the performance of bomber and tank crews. Flanagan observed that, when asked to describe an effective performance, the response was usually a list of vague descriptions such as 'courage', 'leadership', 'know-how' and so on. If pressed to give an example of what he meant the respondent could often provide a specific example and it was these incidents that led Flanagan to invent the term 'critical incident' for a piece of behaviour directly related to effective (or ineffective) job performance.

Critical incidents are valuable as they are *data*, not opinion. Secondly, they can be gathered from a range of different sources, both up and down the hierarchy.

These incidents can then lead directly to the job analysis and the subsequent interview questions. In their book *Behaviour Description Interviewing*, Janz, Hellervik and Gilmore (1986) point out that seeking evidence of local incidents leads directly to two key principles mentioned in *In Search of Excellence* (Peters and Waterman, 1982). These are: (1) productivity through people and (2) closeness to the customer. By enquiring of, and listening to, managers, supervisors and incumbents, the organisation is demonstrating its concern for people. Further, discussions with the customers not only provide information on relevant incidents, but they involve customers in the development of the organisation. And as Leavitt said in a slightly different context, 'people support what they help to create'.

Conducting an analysis of critical incidents

In preparing a critical incident job analysis it is important to concentrate on the *behaviour* of the person. Dr R.F. Mager in a different context (he was writing about training objectives) listed 'words open to many interpretations', and 'words open to fewer interpretations' and suggested that the more one used those words open to fewer interpretations the less likely one was to leave oneself open to misinterpretation. His lists are shown in Table 3.

Table 3 Words — interpretation and misinterpretation (Mager, 1962)

Words open to many interpretations	Words open to fewer interpretations
To know	To write
To understand	To recite
To *really* understand	To identify
To appreciate	To differentiate
To *fully* appreciate	To solve
To grasp the significance of	To construct
To enjoy	To list
To believe	To compare
To have faith in	To contrast

Mager goes on to say,

Although it is all right to include such words as 'understand' and 'appreciate' in a statement, the statement is not explicit enough to be useful until it indicates how you intend to sample the 'understanding' and 'appreciating'. Until you describe what the learner will be *doing* when demonstrating that he 'understands' or 'appreciates' you have described very little at all.'

Janz *et al* similarly emphasise this point. They say: 'Well written incidents avoid such adjectives as *effective, efficient, good, often, sometimes,* and *usually.*'

These incidents can be collected in a variety of ways either from written forms or face-to-face interviews. The latter is generally considered the better.

Janz *et al* suggest that the number of incidents to be collected should be the minimum of 80–100 which are then divided into a number of 'performance dimensions'. That is, the incidents are classified under a number of headings. From these headings it should be possible then to prepare questions for the 'behaviour description' interview. The 'Behaviour dimensions' and 'Interview questions' for a position of Personnel Officer are given in Appendix 4.1 at the end of this chapter.

Users of this highly structured technique believe that, with some training, interviewers can assess candidates on the responses to the questions and *not* on the intuition or hunch. Some believe that this may be no more than adding up the points under the various dimensions; others, reasonably, argue that the dimensions may differ substantially in their importance and thus should be given different weightings. This is a vexed question: a low score on a vital dimension could, theoretically, be outweighed by high scores on all other dimensions. For example the behaviour dimensions for a cashier could include industry, punctuality, neatness, good appearance and numerical skill. A candidate may get a top score on all of these characteristics but have a zero on honesty. Thus, while the overall score could be a high one the candidate clearly would be unsuited to the position. However, provided the interviewer does not become too rigid in the use of summing up of points for the various dimensions, behaviour description interviewing seems likely to lead to better judgements from the interview. Moreover, the supporters of this technique argue that there are real cash benefits from this selection method. Indeed, Janz *et al* use sophisticated statistical techniques far too complex to go into in a book of this nature. For example their formula for calculating savings in dollars is:

$$U = [(t)\,(N_8)\,(r_2 - r_1)\,(SD_y)\,(O/p)] - [(N_8(c_2 - c_1)/p].$$

Where

U = the savings in dollars due to improved interviewing,

t = the tenure of those selected in years,

N_8 = the number of openings,

$r_2 - r_1$ = the improvement in selection accuracy, measured as the population correlation for applicants between performance on the predictor (interview, tests) and performance on the job,

SD_y = the annual standard deviation of performance in dollars,

O/p = the bell-curve advantage that comes from selecting from more than one applicant,

p = the selection ratio (openings divided by number of applicants), and

$c_2 - c_1$ = the difference in the dollar costs of selection per applicant under the traditional versus the behaviour method.

Using such formulae they cite an example of recruitment in a hospital where they expected to appoint some 500 nurses over three years. Having assumed an improved prediction from the existing unstructured interview they calculate that the saving would be in excess of $3 million! (For details and other examples see *Behaviour Description Interviewing* by Janz *et al.*)

Certainly, behaviour description interviewing could be of great value to the relatively untrained, inexperienced interviewer. It is, however, a relatively unsubtle technique and, while effective at junior and middle grade appointments, it would not appear to be suited to the assessment of key people at the top of an organisation. It may be significant that although the structured interview has a long history, it is not widely used.

The panel interview

There are, of course, other wide-ranging types of interview. Perhaps the most widely used (and abused) is the panel interview. Unless this technique is handled with system and skill it is, in the belief of most experts, a far less effective judgement technique than the individual interview. Moreover, there are arguments that board interviews are less relaxed than individual interviews and therefore provide less useful information about the candidate.

In an unstructured panel interview, one in which the members of the panel do not have clearly allotted roles, the session can deteriorate seriously. The author has even seen a panel discussing issues among themselves with such concentration that the candidate was merely an interested observer!

Debates about panel versus individual interview reflect strongly-held views but there is little hard evidence to support either viewpoint. The judgement of most experts, however, comes down heavily in favour of the one-to-one interview. In situations where it appears important that a number of people should meet the candidate, such interviews can be conducted sequentially. In the author's view, it is difficult enough for the candidate to relate to one stranger let alone three, four or perhaps far more. It seems self-evident that if one wishes to conduct an interview in depth, the one-to-one interview has considerable advantages.

Advantages of the panel interview

- Members can discuss observed behaviour and are thus less likely to meet the problems of contradictory findings from sequential interviews.
- Allows all people directly concerned with the appointment to view the candidates (but this can also be done in sequential interviews).
- Emphasises the importance of the occasion.
- Different experts can pose appropriate technical questions.

Disadvantages of the panel interview

- May awe the candidate — difficult to put an individual at ease.
- Makes it difficult for the candidate to present his views in detail.
- If not well-designed and well-controlled can become a muddle.
- Members of the panel may be more concerned to impress their colleagues than learn about the candidate.
- Expensive — involves the time of several senior executives.
- Candidates are less likely to admit to frailties before a group than in discussion with one sympathetic interviewer.

Appendix 4.1
Behaviour dimensions and interview questions for a position of personnel officer (from Janz *et al*, 1986)

Behaviour dimensions

- Works steadily and diligently, manages time and prepares for periods of hectic activity *versus* wastes time, does not plan ahead or schedule work according to hectic and slow times.
- Checks work thoroughly for errors and completeness *versus* makes mistakes.
- Aids and acts on employees' behalf *versus* neglects employee needs and concerns.

● Takes *versus* avoids responsibility for tasks from start to finish.
● Takes initiative to suggest new programmes and solutions *versus* relies on past practice or ideas from others.
● Maintains a clean, orderly *versus* a disorganised, messy work area.
● Communicates clearly, attentively, and politely to co-workers and employees, handles delicate situations with sensitivity, contributes to a positive work environment *versus* is inattentive, rude, or impatient with peers, is insensitive, and causes resentment and dissention in the workplace.

Interview questions

Recent work experience

● *I would like to begin by having you describe and explain your tasks and responsibilities in your last position.*

Some days it seems that everyone has a problem they need solved or a question they need answered. Tell me about a time when you had people waiting to see you because your appointment calendar was overbooked.

- What were the circumstances that led to your being overbooked?
- How did you handle the situation?
- What were the reactions of the people waiting to see you?
- What was your response to them?
- How satisfied was each individual with the time you spent with him or her and the way you resolved his or her problems?
- What steps did you take to reduce the occurrence of this type of situation in the future?

Tell me about the busiest time you experienced recently.

- When did this happen?
- What did you do to prepare yourself for the onslaught?
- How did you know what to expect?
- How did your preparations pay off during the rush?
- Did your supervisor ever mention anything about your ability to handle these busy periods?
- What did he or she say?

Fortunately, we also experience times that are relatively slack. Tell me about a situation in which you had extra time on your hands.

- How slack was it compared to your normal workday?
- What did you do to keep busy during this time?
- What were your co-workers doing during this period?
- Did you ask for other assignments?
- What were these assignments?
- Tell me about another instance.

Describe a time when you implemented a procedure to help make your job run more smoothly.

- What was the procedure?
- How did you go about organising it?
- What was the reaction of your co-workers to this new procedure?
- How did it make the running of your job smoother?
- How did it affect the jobs of others in your department?

Related work habits

- *Now I would like to find out a bit about your success in catching and correcting errors. What do you do that helps you pick out errors?*

Tell me about a time when you saved the company money by detecting an error.

- When did this happen?
- How did you discover the mistake?
- What was the error?
- Who was responsible?
- What did you do to correct the error?
- What steps did you take to avoid such mistakes in the future?
- How could this error have been avoided?

Can you tell me about a time when you made a mistake in calculating accounts for your company savings plan?

- What was the magnitude of the error?
- How was the mistake brought to your attention?
- How did you correct the error?
- What was the response of the employee whose account was incorrect?
- How did you explain the discrepancy to the employee?
- How did you guard against making such mistakes in the future?
- How often do such mistakes occur over the space of a year?

Sometimes, when we are pressed for time, we neglect to check our work to make sure that it is complete as well as correct. Tell me about a time when you were in this situation.

- What were the circumstances that caused you to neglect this task?
- What was the effect of this incident?
- How do you normally go about checking your work for completeness?
- How did you handle any problems that arose from this incident?
- What did you do the next time this situation arose?

● *An important aspect of the Personnel Officer's job is to aid the employees in understanding policies, benefits, and so forth, and sometimes to act on their behalf. What skills do you possess that help you do this?*

Describe a time when you used these skills on behalf of an employee to overturn a decision that was not made in his or her favour.

- What was the decision?
- Who made it?
- What made you decide to get involved?
- How did you intervene in the situation?
- What was the outcome?
- How were your efforts perceived by the employee?
- What did he or she say to you?
- How many times do you become involved in such situations over the period of a year?

Tell me about a time when you aided an employee in understanding a difficult policy.

- What was the policy?
- How did you know that the employee was having trouble understanding?
- What did you do or say that helped?
- How did you know that you had been successful in your attempt?
- What was it about the policy that was difficult?
- What steps did you take to change the policy so that it would be easier for others to understand?

Sometimes, we are asked to make exceptions to the rules. Can you recall a time when an employee approached you for a withdrawal from the savings plan after the deadline had passed?

- What reason did the employee give for missing the deadline?
- What did you do?
- How did the employee react?
- What was the final outcome?
- How did this situation differ from others of a similar nature?
- How frequent are such requests in a 6-month period?

Can you recall the last time you were rushed but took the time to answer an employee's questions regarding material readily available in the company manual?

- What did the employee want to know?
- How did you respond to the request?
- How long did it take you to complete the task?
- How did it affect your other work?
- How often do these types of situations arise within a 6-month period?

Tell me about the last time you handled a housing loan request for an employee.

- What steps did you take in handling the loan?
- How did the way you handled this loan differ from the way you usually handle loans?
- How long did it take?
- What was the employee's response to the way you handled the loan?

- *I would now like to focus more on your work habits. In general, briefly describe how you normally go about accomplishing an assigned task.*

Describe for me the last time you were asked to prepare a presentation on short notice and were given very sketchy details as to required content.

- What was the presentation?
- How did you gather the necessary information to prepare?
- What steps did you go through in organising the task?
- Whom did you get to help you with the task?
- How did you work around the time constraint?
- What sort of feedback did you receive from those who attended the presentation? From your supervisor?
- How would you have organised the presentation if you had had more time?

Can you recall a time when you had to leave a portion of unfinished work in the hands of someone else?

- What were the circumstances that led to the situation?
- How did the other employee react to the extra work?
- What type of instructions did you have to supply to have the task completed?
- What did you do to monitor the progress of the other employee?
- What do you normally do to keep track of the tasks you delegate?
- What comments, if any, did your supervisor make regarding the way the task was accomplished?

Tell me about the last time you undertook a project that demanded a lot of initiative.

- What type of project was it?
- How did you become involved in the project?
- Why was initiative called for?
- What steps did you go through in accomplishing the project?
- What obstacles did you encounter, and how did you overcome them?
- What was the outcome?

In this type of position, there is often a large amount of paperwork and many files. Tell me about a time when you were able to put your hands on what you needed immediately because of your system for organising files.

- What were the circumstances leading up to the situation?
- What information did you need?
- How were you able to get it so quickly?
- How did this affect the outcome?
- How would the outcome have been different if you had not been able to get the information quickly?
- What comments did your supervisor make about the situation and the way you handled it?

Tell me about a time when you were unable to locate certain papers that were important for a major decision.

- What was the decision?
- How did you go about locating the papers?
- Who else was involved in the search?

- How was the decision finally made?
- What steps did you take to avoid this type of situation in the future?

Communication skills

● *Human resource personnel are continually communicating with people in both good and bad situations. What do you feel is your most effective method of communication? Why?*

Tell me about the last time you had a really good idea and had to persuade your supervisor to accept it.

- What was your idea?
- How did you present your idea to your supervisor?
- What did he or she find difficult to accept about your idea?
- What made the situation especially difficult for you?
- What was the outcome?

At times, we have to deal with very fragile emotional situations. Tell me about the last time you had to visit the widow of a deceased employee.

- What was the purpose of your visit?
- How did you feel about the visit?
- What did you do or say to help put the widow at ease?
- How did the widow react to you?
- How did this situation differ from the way you normally handle such matters?
- What was the outcome of the visit?

Can you recall the last time an applicant insisted he or she was the best candidate for a position?

- What was the position?
- What did you say to the applicant?
- How did the applicant react to the rejection?
- What was the outcome of the situation?

Describe a time an employee requested some confidential information from you.

- Who was the person requesting the information?
- What reason did he or she give for wanting the information?

- What did you say to the person?
- What was the response?
- How was the situation eventually handled?
- How did you handle this situation differently from your normal way?
- What comments, if any, did your supervisor make about the situation?
- How has the outcome affected your relationship with the employee who asked for the information?

Working effectively with your co-workers is obviously important. Tell me about a time when you used your social strengths to help your co-workers through a difficult time.

- What were the circumstances leading up to the difficulty?
- What steps did you take to improve the situation?
- What was the result of your efforts?
- How was your relationship with your co-workers affected?
- How often have you helped out in this manner in the past year?

When a group of people work closely together, it is inevitable that conflict will arise. Tell me about the most serious disagreement you have had with a co-worker.

- When did this happen?
- What led to the disagreement?
- How did you attempt to solve the problem?
- What was your co-worker's reaction?
- How was the situation resolved?
- What is your relationship with that person today?
- How often over a period of 6 months did you find yourself in this type of situation?

Further reading

Argyle, M. *The Psychology of Interpersonal Behaviour*, 4th ed, Penguin, Harmondsworth, 1983.

Courtis, J. *Interviews: Skills and Strategy*, IPM, London, 1988.

Eysenck, H.J. *Uses and Abuses of Psychology*, Penguin, Harmondsworth, 1955.

Fear, R.A. *The Evaluation Interview*, McGraw-Hill, New York, 1958.

Fletcher, J. *Effective Interviewing*, Kogan Page, London, 1988.

Higham, M. *The ABC of Interviewing*, IPM, London, 1979.

Janz, T., Hellervik, L. and Gilmore, D.C. *Behaviour Description Interviewing*, Allyn & Bacon, Boston, 1986.

Mackenzie Davey, D. and Harris, M. (eds). *Judging People*, McGraw-Hill, London, 1982.

Mackenzie Davey, D. and McDonnell, P. *How to Interview*, IBM, London, 1975.

Mager, R.F. *Preparing Instructional Objectives*, Fearon, Belmont, California, 1962, 1975.

Peters, T.J. and Waterman R.H. *In Search of Excellence: Lessons from America's Best Run Companies*, Harper & Row, New York, 1982.

Plumbley, P. *Recruitment and Selection*, 4th ed, IPM, London, 1985.

Rodger, A. *The Seven Point Plan*, NIIP, London, 1952.

Sidney, E. (ed) *Managing Recruitment*, Gower, London, 1988.

Sidney, E. and Brown M. *The Skills of Interviewing*, Tavistock, London, 1961.

Chapter 5
Psychological Tests

Psychological tests can be put into a variety of categories. They can, for example, be divided into tests with right answers and tests in which there is no right answer — perhaps better called 'inventories'. Or they could be related to the specific needs of the user. Does he simply wish to find out whether the person has mechanical aptitude? Or can handle numerical problems with speed and accuracy? Or whether he is emotionally tough enough to withstand a particularly stressful job? And there is the user who, in the broadest terms, tries to answer, reasonably comprehensively, two questions:

1. How able is this person?
2. What kind of person is she or he?

Such an approach would be important, for example, in career guidance.

Another approach is to examine the questions posed in a structured interviewing approach (See Chapter 4) and considering where tests can contribute to answers, often by giving far more objective measures of the characteristics being considered. Rodger Holdsworth adopts this approach in his useful booklet *Personnel Selection Testing — A Guide for Managers*. He points out that useful classification is to describe tests under the headings of the Seven Point Plan (see Table 2, p. 70). Holdsworth points out that tests exist for all points in the plan except 'circumstances'. He does, of course, include the qualification that some areas can be tested more adequately than others. Moreover, Alec Rodger himself pointed out that in using the plan the weight attached to any particular heading will depend on the purpose for which it is being used.

A similar structure is adopted here although the order has been changed starting with what many people would consider the most valuable aids to judgement: the testing of intelligence. Few would argue that intelligence testing is a better developed and more sophisticated area of technology than is, for example, the assessment of interests, although it could reasonably be argued that a knowledge of a candidate's level of intelligence could be of minor importance in certain jobs.

Even experienced interviewers
can be influenced by
irrelevant factors

Intellectual tests

Tests of general intelligence

The nature of intelligence is discussed in Chapter 7 where it is suggested that intelligence is, in non-technical terms, 'the ability to solve problems', 'the ability to understand cause and effect', and 'the ability to examine a seemingly disparate range of issues and integrate them into a meaningful whole'. Given these definitions it seems self-evident that some knowledge of the *degree* to which any individual has this talent will be helpful in understanding him.

Although in day-to-day meetings people will generally be classified as 'bright' or 'dull', 'intellectual' or 'non-intellectual', these subjective judgements have been shown to be to a very large degree, faulty. Even experienced interviewers can be influenced by a number of irrelevant factors when assessing intelligence: people who are fluent are rated as having higher IQs than those who are inarticulate; those who look agreeable are ranked higher than those who look disagreeable; those who wear glasses tend to be thought of as more intelligent than those who do not! While, of course, in many situations (for example, most social encounters) it is not possible to apply an intelligence test, in many others, such as selecting students or trainees, engaging new employees or selecting people for promotion, it seems perverse to use guesswork where well-developed objective measuring instruments are available. (If it were judged important to know the weight of an individual it would be absurd to guess and not use a scale.) And, while tests of intelligence are nothing like as accurate as good weighing machines, they can remove a great deal of subjectivity. They have, after all, been used for most of this century and they can, in a relatively short period, provide accurate information about the intellectual capacity of the individual. (Again, as indicated in Chapter 7, *having* the capacity does not necessarily mean putting it to efficient use — just as knowing the cubic capacity of an engine of a vehicle alone will not give any precise information about how fast it can travel, how heavy a load it can carry or what gradient it can climb. It could, however, be a good starting point if establishing such matters were of importance.)

What are tests of intelligence like? They can consist of items in a particular medium such as words or very often of a mixture of various media — words, numbers and abstract diagrams. These tests are usually carried out under pressure of time. This practice is administratively convenient — one cannot, in practice, allow a job candidate (for example) an unlimited time to solve the problems in any particular test. It has been argued that time limits are intrinsically unfair. Some psychologists assert that there should be two factors, one of *power* and one of *speed*. The majority of psychologists, however, accept that people who can do these tests well can do them quickly. And, indeed, most of the experimental work confirms this view.

Verbal tests*. Verbal tests include pure vocabulary tests, usually given in multi-choice form, for example:

(a) Which of the following words means the same as 'sick':
    (i) cool (ii) green (iii) ill (iv) rough (v) short

A more difficult example is:

(b) Which of the following words mean the same as 'extirpate':
    (i) banish (ii) discover (iii) destroy (iv) defrock (v) forgive

*Correct answers are given in Appendix 5.1 at the end of this Chapter.

The same type of item can be put in a less direct form:

(c) What word can mean both 'sound of a dog' and 'outside of a tree'?

Or perhaps, more difficult:

(d) What word can mean 'signify' and 'ignoble'?

Perhaps even trickier is the format used in the 'pairs' test. In this, the candidate is presented with five words and told that among them will be two pairs and thus one odd man out. For example:

(e) Groove
     Small
     Ridge
     Fixed
     Tiny

Or perhaps more difficult:

(f) Maudlin
     Volatile
     Lenient
     Discreet
     Eternal

Analogies are also used in verbal tests, for example:

(g) 'Summer' is to 'winter' as 'hot' is to:
     (i) bath (ii) cold (iii) heat (iv) spring

Or again, more difficult:

(h) 'Etiolate' is to 'illuminate' as 'blanch' is to:
     (i) encourage (ii) display (iii) tan (iv) lighten (v) harden

A list of some established verbal tests is given in Appendix 5.2.

Numerical tests. Number series are commonly used in non-verbal tests, for example:

(a) Fill in the missing number in the series below:
    9   7   5   *   1

and very much more difficult:

(b) 98   63   37   19   *   3

Arithmetical/mathematical problems are also used, for example:

(c) Three pencils cost 27p. What would eight pencils cost?
    (i) 80p
    (ii) 76p
    (iii) 72p
    (iv) 78p
    (v) 69p

Or

(d) A bus left the terminus at 8 a.m. on an outgoing trip which covered 27 miles. After waiting 30 minutes it began its return journey. On the outgoing trip it averaged 18 miles per hour. On the return it averaged 50 per cent faster. What time did it arrive at the terminus?

  (i) 10.40 a.m.

 (ii) 11.00 a.m.

(iii) 11.20 a.m.

(iv) 11.40 a.m.

 (v) 12.00 noon

Some established numerical tests are listed in Appendix 5.2.

Abstract reasoning tests. Also found are a series of diagrammatic/ symbolic tests which were initially devised to overcome the problems of language and differences in culture. While there is some evidence to suggest that they do by-pass the language problem in a relatively unified culture, such as the western world, they are by no means culture-free and cannot, for example, be used to make direct comparisons between illiterate and literate, Africans and Europeans or, say, Orientals and Americans. This has become an issue of great importance in the world of psychological testing. Examples of the typical problems are given in Figure 7. Some established tests of abstract reasoning are given in Appendix 5.2.

Matrices — Which of the numbered squares should be in the square marked ⊡

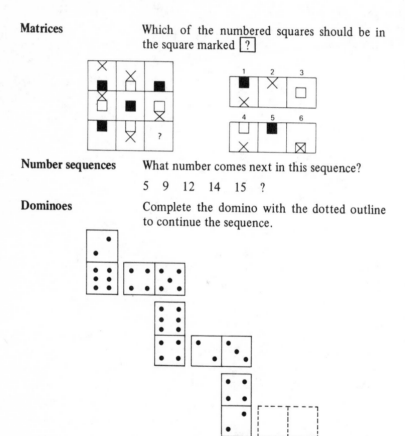

Number sequences — What number comes next in this sequence?

5   9   12   14   15   ?

Dominoes — Complete the domino with the dotted outline to continue the sequence.

Figure 7 Typical abstract reasoning tests.

General intelligence tests. These tests are generally made up from a mixture of items from the categories above. Examples are given in Appendix 5.2 and catalogues from test agencies will provide information on a range of intelligence and other tests.

Tests of applied intelligence

Logical skills. Attempts have been made to see how well people can use their intelligence in examining issues logically and objectively. Perhaps the best known of these tests is the Watson Glaser Critical Thinking Appraisal. This aims to give a measure of the total concept of critical thinking by the use of five sub-tests. The five tests are:

TEST 1 — INFERENCE: discriminating among degree of truth or falsity of inferences drawn from given data.

TEST 2 — RECOGNITION OF ASSUMPTIONS: recognising unstated assumptions or presuppositions of given statements or assertions.

TEST 3 — DEDUCTION: determining whether certain conclusions necessarily follow from information given in statements or premises.

TEST 4 — INTERPRETATION: weighing evidence and deciding if generalisations or conclusions based on the given data are warranted.

TEST 5 — EVALUATION OF ARGUMENTS: distinguishing between arguments that are strong and relevant and those that are weak or irrelevant to a particular question at issue.

Imaginative thinking. Various, not wholly successful, attempts have been made to establish the degree to which an individual can think creatively or imaginatively. Many of these are versions of the '*How many uses can you think of for a brick?*' type. Candidates are faced with unlikely, even bizzare, assumptions and asked to suggest what the consequences would be politically, socially and economically. For example, '*What would happen if, perhaps due to nuclear leakage, all children were born with a third arm emerging from the middle of their chest.*' Or '*What would happen if some astronomical changes resulted in the disappearance of the day and night cycle and we remained permanently fixed at midday?*' It is difficult to quantify the scoring of these tests but experienced observers can make useful comparisons on both quantity and quality of ideas.

Attempts have been made to design more quantifiable tests. In the following example candidates are given something like Figure 8 and an instruction such as, 'on this page are some meaningless lines or figures. You are to add a few lines to each to make it a meaningful drawing and write under it what it is supposed to be. You have four minutes to do as many as you can. Start now.' The score is simply based on the number completed.

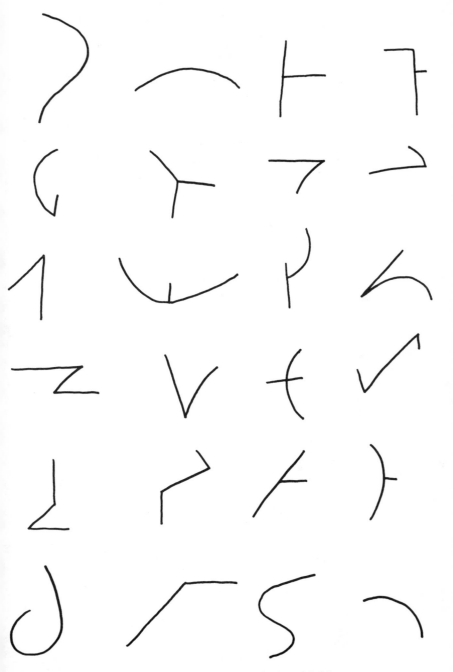

Figure 8 An example of an imaginative thinking test.

Aptitude tests

Engineering aptitude. Engineering — or mechanical — aptitude appears to be very largely based on how movement has been transferred. However, because this is closely related to general intelligence, it is difficult to measure this aptitude in isolation. Groups of tests (known as 'batteries') have, however, been designed and do appear to predict success in, for example, mechanical engineering reasonably well. These batteries usually include some spatial aptitude tests. Figure 9 is an example of a mechanical comprehension test.

As indicated above mechanical aptitude test batteries generally include spatial aptitude tests in which tests assess the ability to manipulate shapes and sizes, for example Figure 10.

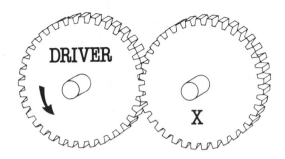

What will happen to the wheel X
when the driver turns as shown?

    (i)   Turn the same way _____

    (ii)   Turn the opposite way _____

    (iii)   Move to and fro _____

    (iv)   Cannot tell _____

    (v)   The mechanism will jam _____

Which of these children balanced on the
seesaw weighs the heaviest?

    (i)   F _____

    (ii)   G _____

    (iii)   H _____

    (iv)   All equal _____

    (v)   Cannot tell _____

Figure 9 A typical mechanical comprehension test.

HOW TO DO THE TEST

This test is to see how well you can judge shapes. Each item consists of three shapes exactly the same, but one of them has been turned over. Your task is to find out which shape is turned over. What you have to do is explained below.

First look at these three letters. They are all the same except that the third one is turned over.

P   P   q

Now look at each of these rows and find the letter or shape that has been turned over.

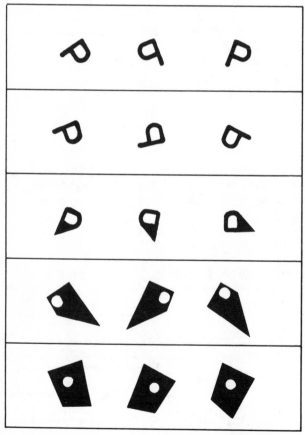

Figure 10 A typical spatial aptitude test.

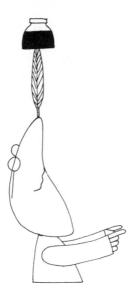

Clerical aptitude. In the past a large number of clerical jobs called upon an ability to check and classify words, figures and symbols. While there may still be a number of tasks where these skills are important they are diminishing and far more important in the office of today is the ability to gain some skill in the various aspects of using computers. Figure 11 is an example of the classical clerical aptitude test.

Newer tests in this field include aptitude tests for word-processor operators, computer programers and even language aptitude tests — attempts to assess the capacity for learning languages.

Aptitude for complex skills. For certain highly complex tasks elaborate combinations of tests have been used to predict success. One of the most prominent and most successful of these, largely developed during the Second World War, was a battery of tests designed to measure the ability to learn to fly an aircraft. In peacetime, one can usually choose people who are likely to gain this skill in a reasonably short period. During war, however, it may often be necessary to change the level of intake depending upon whether there is a shortage of pilots or a shortage of aircraft. Should it be the latter one could limit the intake to the flying training course to those of the highest aptitude. In the former case standards could be dropped but one would know that, even among those with lower aptitude, there would be some who could

Educational and Industrial Test Services Ltd

Clerical Test 1
Speed and Accuracy

NAME _____ AGE _____

HOW TO DO THE TEST

There are two parts to this test.

The first part consists of pairs of numbers, like this.

Your task is to check the pair of numbers to see whether they are the same or different. If the two numbers are exactly the SAME, put a tick through the S between them. If the two numbers are DIFFERENT, put a tick through the D.

Now do the Practice Test below in the same way. Work quickly but carefully.

PRACTICE TEST

32	S D	34
93	S D	93
516	S D	536
5893	S D	5839
1776	S D	1776

The second part consists of pairs of names. Your task is to check these to see whether they are the same or different. If the two names of the pair are EXACTLY the same, put a tick through the S. If the two names are different, put a tick through the D. In the practice test below the names in the first pair are <u>different</u>.

Now do this practice test in the same way.

PRACTICE TEST

George Hall	S D	Geo. Hall
J. Smith	S D	P. Smith
John Harris	S D	John Harris
Longman & Co.	S D	Longmans & Co.
Peters Ltd.	S D	Peters Ltd.
Paul Baker	S D	Paul Barker

The two parts of the test over the page are done like these. You will be told when to begin. Work quickly but carefully.

YOU WILL BE TOLD WHEN TO TURN OVER

Prepared and distributed by
EDUCATIONAL AND INDUSTRIAL TEST SERVICES LTD
Hemel Hempstead, Hertfordshire, England
Copyright © 1983, E.I.T.S. Ltd

Figure 11 A typical clerical aptitude test.

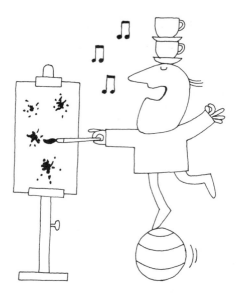

become successful pilots. This can be neatly illustrated in an 'Expectancy chart' (see Figure 12) in which even in the lowest-grade 18 per cent will pass the flying test.

Overall aptitude tests grading	Percentage chance of passing flying test
A = Top 10%	83
B = Next 20%	65
C = Middle 40%	55
D = Next 20%	37
E = Bottom 10%	18

Figure 12 An expectancy chart.

133

Achievement/attainment tests

As the name suggests these are instruments designed to make more objective assessments of either what a person knows or what he can do. School and college examinations are examples of this type of test and the range is almost endless: mathematics, typing, shorthand, engineering knowledge, etc. While a great deal can, of course, be learned from a person's background, qualifications and work experience, such pointers can be misleading: qualifications can become dated and experience irrelevant. Indeed, one of the great problems in many fields is keeping up to date with the explosion of knowledge. A highly-qualified and long-experienced engineer, for example, may have failed to have kept up with the latest developments. On the other hand, people with limited education and no qualifications in languages may have become skilled linguists — or highly proficient users of their own language.

While test catalogues will often list attainment tests many organisations find it a relatively simple matter to design instruments which can be applied to incoming candidates. Security can pose a problem with such tests. That is, candidates can discover what is to be asked, prepare answers and so invalidate the assessment. One way to circumvent this weakness is to change the tests regularly but this, as with most academic examinations, leaves the problem of standardisation.

Achievement tests are generally used in association with other tests of general ability, aptitude and personality.

Personality tests

Before moving on to the question of whether one can 'measure' personality — and if so how — it is important to define it. In popular use, 'personality' can be used as a synonym for charm, attractiveness and social presence — 'Cynthia has personality'. Indeed, the word has become a synonym for a celebrity — a famous name or star. However, while psychologists can be dismissive about this use of the term, they still find it very difficult to define what they mean. In a notably impressive book by Allport published in 1937 he offered some fifty definitions of personality almost concluding with a beautifully simple expression 'what a man really is'. Arthur Reber in his *Dictionary of Psychology* (1985) avoids definition and discusses personality in terms of 'type theories' and similar approaches, such as those discussed in Chapter 1. Yet, even after two pages in his dictionary, he admits that his discussion 'does not, of course, exhaust the theoretical approaches that have had their turn in the scientific spotlight'.

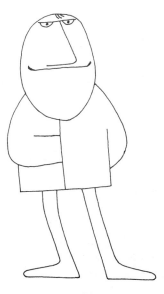

Here we shall use the term to cover almost all the individual characteristics not covered by the cognitive factors discussed earlier in this chapter. These would include emotional adjustment, motivation, interest, attitudes and values. (It might be circumspect to note here that Sarah Hampson argues that the assumption that 'personality' is something that each individual has is open to challenge. Indeed, she argues that it is not a property possessed exclusively by individuals but rather something created as a result of individuals reacting with each other. 'It is through the social process that we construct the personalities of ourselves and others'.)

In this chapter, however, we are concerned more with the tests and how well they do what they purport to do rather than with the theories.

Personality questionnaires/inventories

Perhaps the most widely used and best known of personality questionnaires is Cattell's 16 personality factors (PF). As the name suggests this provides scores on 16 personality traits. Scores are derived from the answers to such questions as:

I like to watch team games

A. Yes
B. Occasionally
C. No

Money cannot bring happiness

A. Yes (true)
B. In between
C. No (false)

Forms A and B each have 187 such items.

The 16PF is especially popular in the United Kingdom perhaps largely because there is a range of courses which trains the non-psychologist in its use. Thus many personnel managers, counsellors, teachers etc, have used the test. The sixteen personality factors were in the main given special names (see the terms in brackets in Figure 13). Psychologists face the dilemma of whether to devise and use jargon terms or use commonplace words. Even something as seemingly straightforward as 'intelligence' suffers from this. Many psychologists, in order to be precise in their usage, insist on refering to 'g' (the general factor of intelligence identified and called 'g' by Spearman) but when asked what they mean by 'g' have to answer *'Well, general intelligence'* only to be met with the response *'Well, if you mean intelligence, why don't you say so?'* Cattell, it seems suffered in the same way and eventually resorted to 'plain English' descriptive terms to describe his factors.

There are similar instruments. The Minnesota Multi-phasic Personality Inventory (MMPI) was one of the earliest inventories and was designed essentially for psychiatric use. It is long (550 questions, many of which are intrusive and which can offend some subjects).

The Eysenck Personality Inventory is a relatively short test (57 items) measuring introversion/extraversion and stability/neuroticism. It is not widely used in — and nor was it designed for — personnel work although it appears to generate a number of predictions relevant to working life. For example, extraverts appear to lack persistence with repetitive tasks and thus will be less satisfied in clerical jobs.

The Guilford Zimmerman Temperament Survey provides measures on 10 personality factors shown in Figure 14.

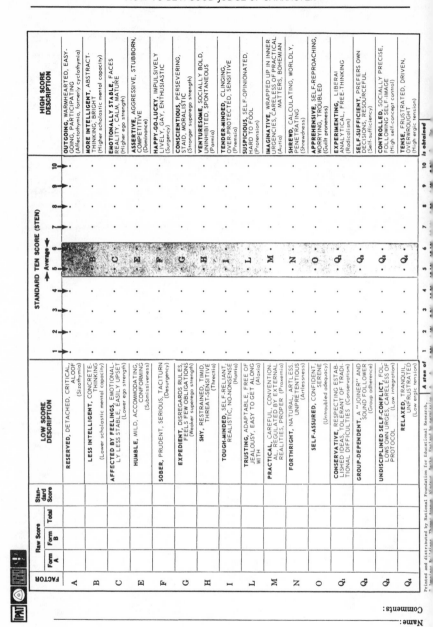

Figure 13 16PF test profile

PROFILE CHART FOR THE GUILFORD-ZIMMERMAN TEMPERAMENT SURVEY
For high-school, college, and adult ages

C SCORE	G General Activity Energy	R Restraint Seriousness	A Ascendance Social Boldness (M)	(F)	S Social Interest Sociability	E Emotional Stability	O Objectivity	F Friendliness Agreeableness (M)	(F)	T Thoughtfulness Reflectiveness	P Personal Relations Cooperativeness	M Masculinity Femininity (M)	(F)	CENTILE RANK	NEAREST T SCORE
10	30 29 28	30 29 28 27	30 29 28	30 29 28 27	30	30 29	30 29	30 28 26	30 29 28	30 29 28	30 29	30 29	0 1	99	75
9	27 26	26 25	27 26	26 25 24	29	28 27	28 27	25 24	27 26	27 26	28 27	28 27	2 3		70
8	25 24	24 23	25 24	23 22 21	28 27	26 25	26 25	23 22 21	25 24	25 24	26 25	26 25	4 5	95 90	65
7	23 22	22 21	23 22 21	20 19	26 25	24 23	24 23	20 19	23 22 21	23 22	24 23	24	6 7	80	60
6	21 20	20 19 18	20 19 18	18 17 16	24 23 22	22 21 20	22 21 20	18 17 16	20 19 18	21 20	22 21 20	23 22	8 9	70 60	55
5	19 18 17	17 16 15	17 16 15	15 14 13	21 20 19	19 18 17	19 18 17	15 14 13	17 16 15	19 18 17	19 18 17	21 20	10 11	50 40	50
4	16 15 14	14 13 12	14 13 12	12 11	18 17 16 15	16 15 14 13	16 15 14	12 11 10	14 13 12	16 15 14	16 15 14	19 18	12 13	30	45
3	13 12 11	11 10	11 10	10 9 8	14 13 12 11	12 11 10 9	13 12 11 10	9 8 7	11 10 9	13 12 11	13 12	17 16 15	14 15	20	40
2	10 9 8	9 8 7	9 8 7	7 6	10 9 8 7	8 7 6	9 8 7	6 5	8 7	10 9 8	11 10 9	14 13 12	16 17 18	10 5	35
1	7 6	6 5	6 5	5 4 3	6 5 4	5 4	6 5	4 3	6 5	7 6 5	8 7 6	11 10 9	19 20		30
0	5 3 2 1	4 3 2 1	4 3 2 1	2 1 0	3 2 1 0	3 2 1	4 3 2 1	2 1 0	4 3 2 1	4 3 2 1	5 3 1	8 5 2	21 23 25	1	25

	M F						M F				M F	
Inactivity Slowness	Impulsiveness Rhathymia	Submissiveness		Shyness Seclusiveness	Emotional Instability Depression	Subjectivity Hypersensitiveness	Hostility Belligerence		Unreflectiveness	Criticalness Intolerance	Femininity	Masculinity

Figure 14 The Guilford Zimmerman Temperament Survey

The California Personality Inventory gives measures on 22 personality traits. It is far more acceptable than the MMPI — indeed, it is sometimes called 'the sane man's MMPI'.

The Myers Briggs Type Indicator — again a long-established test based on Jung's theory types is still well thought of and reasonably widely used. (An example of the use of this instrument is given in Chapter 2.)

The Occupational Personality Questionnaire (OPQ) has been developed and published in the United Kingdom by Saville & Holdsworth. It was designed specifically to assess personality characteristics relevant in the world of work, assessment and counselling. There are 10 different versions, with various response formats used for each version. Some therefore are more suitable for selection purposes, others for counselling. The main domains of personality measured by the OPQ are: relationships with people; thinking style; and feelings and emotions. The longest form, the Concept Model (see Table 4) assesses 30 primary factors and takes about 60 minutes to complete, or the shortest, Pentagon measures five dimensions and takes about 10 minutes. There are also Factor and Oregon measures.

The cost of using the OPQ is high involving a licence of about £1000 a year on top of costs of materials and training.

Projective tests

Projective tests are based on the hypothesis that the different responses made by different people to precisely the same stimulus must reflect differences in their personalities. For example, shown an ink blot (as in the Rorschach Test, see Figure 16) or a picture (as in Murray's Thermatic Apperception Test) the candidate is asked to tell a story or describe his responses. Some attempts have been made at objective scoring of responses but on the whole the psychologist uses his intuition to make judgements of various motives, attitudes and beliefs of the patient or candidate.

If there is value in projective tests then it is certainly only in the hands of psychologists with extensive experience in the use of these instruments.

Table 4 The three forms of the Occupational Personality Questionnaires: Factors, Octagon and Pentagon, which measure fifteen, eight
and five traits (Saville & Holdsworth Ltd, 1985). (Reproduced by
permission.)

OPQ FACTOR MODEL	OCTAGON MODEL	PENTAGON MODEL
People		
Influence	Assertive	
Social confidence		
Empathy	Empathy	Extraversion
Gregarious	Gregarious	
Social desirability		
Cognitive style		
Imaginative	Abstract	Abstract
Conservative		
Planful	Methodical	Methodical
Detail conscious		
Emotions		
Relaxed	Relaxed	Emotional
Phlegmatic		stability
Optimistic	Self-controlled	
Vigour		
Contesting		
Active	Vigorous	Vigorous
Decisive		

Using and interpreting personality tests

Many attempts have been made to produce personality profiles for
various jobs based on scores from personality tests. This approach has
some strengths but many weaknesses. It is a truism that there is no one
right way of doing any job. And, indeed, the examination of successful
people in any job will often reveal wide-ranging different personalities. Even in something as seemingly straightforward as, say, selling
insurance, one finds very different levels of ability and different types
of personality. Thus, even if it is accepted that personality tests are
valid measures of the individual's traits, the judge is still left with the
problem of deciding whether a particular 'personality' is appropriate
for a particular role. This can be influenced by such factors as the

people he will be operating with or under, or the type of people he may need to supervise.

Another danger of seeking the ideal profile is that it may even screen out the type of person you require. Consider the possibility that successful child psychologists can be divided into two main types. First, the introvert who has some difficulty in relating to other adults but who appears to be able to deal with children in a confidential and trusted way. Secondly, the marked extravert, relaxed in every social situation, who will also deal well with children. If one then averaged out the successful child psychologists one would end up with a profile suggesting that the ideal psychologist would be neither extravert nor introvert — exactly the type one did not want!

Another problem in the use of personality tests is the question of faking. Personality tests are falsifiable — and frequently falsified. This may be done deliberately in an attempt to present the personality the subject believes to be desirable or it may even be an unconscious protest. (The person who fears he may be rather weak and submissive can protest too much and so present himself as extremely domineering). There are, in most personality inventories 'lie detector' or 'falsification' scores. These are sometimes relatively transparent items such as '*I have never told a lie to get myself out of a difficult situation*' or '*I have never been late for an interview*'. (People who agree with these assertions are presumed to be lying.) Yet, in falsifying, people can often provide the judge with useful information. If, for example, an evidently quiet, shy, rather withdrawn person answers test questions in such a way as to show him to be a marked extravert, one could draw some useful conclusions. It may pose the hypothesis that he lacks insight or — and perhaps more likely — that he is well aware that he has some difficulties in relating to others and would prefer (and would like others to think) that this were not the case.

Personality tests, then, set up hypotheses which have to be interpreted by the user. Some of these are discussed in Chapter 7 in examining the problems facing a psychologist conducting full assessment programmes.

How useful are psychological tests?

A cautionary note: psychological tests cannot be evaluated on appearance. Tests with high 'face validity' (that is, they look as if they should measure the quality they purport to measure) often have low real validity; other tests which may not look superficially plausible may prove to be accurate predictors of future behaviour. Thus, in considering the use of the test, the buyer should evaluate the statistical evidence rather than simply examine the instrument. The questions to be asked are: 'What is the evidence that shows that this test measures what it claims to measure?' and 'what is the evidence that it does this consistently?'

Overall, provided one works with the respectable tests (such as those mentioned in this chapter) one can feel reasonably confident that intelligence tests will give a sound measure of intelligence. Aptitude tests too, have a reasonably high predictive value. Achievement tests can give sound objective measures of an individual's level of attainment in a particular area.

As indicated, personality tests are far more complicated and call for very careful interpretation by trained and experienced users. They are probably best left to psychologists who have specialised in that particular field.

Other problems related to the use of psychological tests — especially in the field of employment — can involve legislation, particularly that concerned with unfair discrimination. If tests are to be used in the judgement of potential employees, then the users must ensure that the choice of test be based on the requirements of the job to be filled, and that the chosen tests will not result in discrimination on the basis of sex or ethnic origin. In summary, one must ensure that the tests are effective and fair.

Appendix 5.1
Answers to test questions

Verbal tests
(a) (iii)
(b) (iii)
(c) Bark
(d) Mean
(e) Fixed
(f) Lenient
(g) cold
(h) tan

Numerical tests
(a) 3
(b) 8
(c) (iii)
(d) (ii)

Abstract reasoning tests (Figure 7)
(a) 1
(b)

Mechanical aptitude (Figure 9)
(a) (ii)
(b) (i)

Appendix 5.2
Examples of tests

Verbal tests

Verbal reasoning from DATB
Verbal skill from Morrisby (GAT-V)
Saville Holdsworth BTS
Guilford Zimmerman Verbal Comprehension
NIIP Group Tests 90A and 90B

Numerical tests

Numerical reasoning DATB
Numerical scale Morrisby (GAT-N)
Saville & Holdsworth NT2
Flanagan Mathematical and Reasoning
Guilford Zimmerman General Reasoning
NIIP Test EA2
NIIP Group Test 66

Abstract reasoning tests

Raven's Standard Progressive Matrices
Raven's Advanced Progressive Matrices

Morrisby Compound Series Test
Penrose Dominoes

General intelligence tests

AH2/AH3/AH4/AH5 — These tests were designed by Alice Heim to
   measure ability at increasingly higher levels
Thurstone Test of Mental Alertness
Wonderlic Test
MD5 — a general intelligence test which is easily administered, scored and
   interpreted which has been shown to have a wide range (shop assistants to
   graduates). The test time is 15 minutes.

Mechanical comprehension tests

A typical mechanical comprehension test is that designed by GK Bennett.
Other examples are Morrisby Mechanical Aptitude Test and the Engineering
Apprentice Aptitude Test Battery designed by NIIP.

Spatial aptitude tests

Examples of such tests are the Morrisby Shapes Test, NIIP Group Test 80A,
81 & 82, and Form Relations Test and the famous revised Minnisota Paper
Form Board.

Clerical aptitude tests

Examples of such tests are NIIP Group Test 20, ACER Speed and Accuracy
Test, NIIP Group Test 61.

Appendix 5.3
List of test agencies

EITS
Educational and Industrial Test Services Limited
83 High Street
Hemel Hempstead
Herts HP1 3AH

NFER-NELSON
The NFER-NELSON Publishing Company Limited
Darville House
2 Oxford Road East
Windsor
Berks SL4 1DF

SHL
Saville and Holdsworth Limited
The Old Post House
31 High Street
Esher
Surrey KT10 9QA

SRA
Science Research Associates Limited
Newtown Road
Henley on Thames
Oxon RG9 1EW

The Psychological Corporation
Foots Cray High Street
Sidcup
Kent DA14 5HP

The Test Agency
Cournswood House
North Dean
High Wycombe
Bucks HP14 4NW

Further reading

Aiken, L. R. *Psychological Testing and Assessment*, 6th edn, Allyn & Bacon, Boston, 1988.

Cattell, R.B. *The Scientific Analysis of Personality*, Penguin, Harmondsworth, 1965.

Cook, M. *Personal Selection and Productivity*, John Wiley, Chichester, 1988.

Cronbach, L.J. *Essentials of Psychological Testing*, 4th edn, Harper & Row, New York, 1984.

Guion, R.M. *Personal Testing*, McGraw-Hill, New York, 1965.

Holdsworth, R.F. *Personnel Selection Testing: A Guide for Managers*, BIM, London, 1972.

Miller, K.M. (ed.). *Psychological Testing in Personnel Assessment*, Gower Press, Essex, 1975.

Smith, M. and Robertson, I.T. *Systematic Staff Selection*, Macmillan, London, 1986.

Toplis, J., Dulewicz, V. and Fletcher, C. *Psychological Testing: A Practical Guide for Employers*, IPM, London, 1987.

Chapter 6
Biodata

The best predictor of future performance is past performance. That is, if you wish to know how a person is likely to behave in the future, find out how he or she has behaved in the past. If, for example, a job candidate has changed positions every two years over the last twenty years it is not unreasonable to assume that his next move will be in about two years time. Similarly if he has left jobs because of a personality clash with his boss there is a high likelihood that this too will recur. More positively if the person has a steady record of success in his particular field of sales, such success is likely to continue.

The most widely used method of gathering information about the past is the interview. There is also, however, the use of the biographical data on application forms. Today's fashionable abbreviation for the systematic use of biographical data is 'biodata'. The insurance industry has a notable record in this field. It began in the early 1920s when DB Goldsmith investigated the selection of people selling life insurance — a field in which there was an exceptionally high percentage of failures. Goldsmith took 50 good, 50 average and 50 poor salesmen from a large group and analysed their application forms. These forms provided information on age, marital status, education, occupation, experience of selling insurance, membership of clubs, whether the candidate had applied for full- or part-time selling, whether the candidate himself had life insurance and *whether* (not *what*) the candidate replied to a question '*What amount of insurance are you confident of placing each month?*' He was able to show that the systematic use of this information distinguished between the three groups of salesmen. He then devised scoring systems which involved giving different weights to, a range of answers provided on the form. The scoring for age, for example, was:

18–20 years	–2	30–40 years	+3
21–22 years	–1	41–50 years	+1
23–24 years	0	51–60 years	0
25–27 years	+1	Over 60 years	–1
28–29 years	+2		

*The best predictor of future
performance is past performance*

Education and other factors were given the same asymmetric scoring. Thus Goldsmith converted a conventional application form into what he called a Weighted Application Blank. This principle is well known in other areas of the world of insurance: for example, companies know from their statistics that certain types of driver have more accidents than others and have thus either been refused insurance or charged a higher premium. It should be noted here that the approach is essentially empirical and not logical. It may be less than surprising to discover that young drivers of sports cars have more accidents than older people, or even that people in the entertainment industry or the licensed trades are at greater risk. But why should furriers, or those engaged with the clothing trade, be greater risks as drivers? Or those with vehicles of American or Canadian manufacture? (These latter groups are deemed unacceptable risks by at least one insurance company — presumably on the basis of their statistical evidence.) This pure empiricism may offend some of the more curious users who would like to understand some of the more bizarre findings. For example, they would like to know *why*, say, Siamese cat owners make honest employees. The user of biodata, however, is content with the fact that the scores tend to be reliable predictors. Moreover, because there is no obvious logic to the conclusions, it is very difficult for the applicant to fake. In this field there are distinct advantages over personality tests. Moreover, most responses are verifiable — even if some could take a good deal of time and trouble. Figure 15 provides impressive evidence of the success of Goldsmith's approach.

People in advertising and marketing make similar use of biographical data by classifying the population into economic groups based on their address, whether they have their own telephone, the type of car they own, etc.

The Weighted Application Blank has been used over a wide range of positions from relatively humble jobs to senior management positions. Towards the lower end of the scale, for example, is the example of using a Weighted Application Blank to reduce staff turnovers in pea-canners. The Green Giant Company found that its seasonal pea- and corn-canners often left, seemingly inexplicably, within a few days of starting work, causing the company inconvenience and expense. It was found that the stable production worker lived locally, had a telephone, was married without children, was not an ex-serviceman, was neither under 25 nor over 55, weighed more than 150

Rating-score category	Success rate		
37–39			42%
33–36		31%	
29–32	28%		
25–28	24%		
20–24	11%		

Figure 15 The success of life insurance agents in relationship to scores. (Life Assurance Agency Management Association. From Research Report 1963–1, LIAMA 1963.)

lb but less than 175 lb, had had more than 10 years education, had worked for Green Giant, was able to work to the end of summer, and preferred outside to inside work. From that information it was a relatively straightforward matter to design an application form which would help identify workers who would stay.

At the other end of the scale, a detailed biographical survey was used as the basis for predicting managerial success in Standard Oil of New Jersey. In this research, items reflecting age or experience were eliminated. It was found that successful executives were good in college, pursued leadership opportunities and saw themselves as dominant, assertive and strong. Typically, some of the items were relatively familiar and understandable. Positive scores were rewarded for a stable career without regular job changes, for being married, belonging to clubs and similar organisations and taking an active part in sporting activities. Others were less obvious. Why, for example, should an employee who 'doesn't want a relative contacted in case of an emergency' be a predictor of theft? And, even more puzzling, theft was also likely in candidates who gave no middle initial.

While the early work on biodata was done on conventional application forms it soon became sensible — even necessary — to design special forms, often in a multiple choice questionnaire format. Indeed, The American Psychological Association published a catalogue of life history items (by Glenn, Albright and Owens). This provided such questions as:

'How old was your father when you were born?'
  (i) about 20
 (ii) about 25
(iii) about 30
 (iv) about 35
  (v) don't know

This type of biographical inventory has been used over such diverse jobs as unskilled labourers and research scientists. The most frequent use, however, has been in the selection of sales staff (or, more often, for the rejection of candidates likely to fail in a selling career).

It will be clear that the new type of Weighted Application Blank or Biodata Questionnaire begins to resemble many personality questionnaires. And, indeed, there can be a degree of overlap.

While personality questionnaires are not generally related to particular jobs but designed to give measures of various personality traits they can be used, as is biodata, to be scored for a particular job or group of jobs. For example, in one organisation, a statistical analysis of personality test findings showed a correlation between certain traits and 'survival' — people who stayed. (Unfortunately in this particular study it was also discovered that the people who stayed were not the ones the company wished to keep. Abler employees with greater initiative and drive left to join other organisations.)

Validity

Initial examination of the evidence provides impressive evidence of validity of biodata. However, when the original biodata questionnaire is transferred to employees in seemingly similar organisations there is often a rather more disappointing level of prediction. Moreover, it would appear that changes can take place which can invalidate the original questionnaires. In consequence, they may have to be re-written or at least given new scoring weights. The factors influencing biodata predictors adversely can be changes in the general culture (people in general may be spending more years in education, getting married later, changing jobs more frequently and so on.) There can also, of course, be changes in the nature of the work. A biodata questionnaire which was identifying managers who were appropriate for conditions in 1965 may be quite wrong in identifying the manager for the 1990s.

In an attempt to compare the value of selection methods Hunter and Hunter produced a ranking which produced biodata third after ability tests and job try-outs — still well above the interview — and, of course, far better than astrology, palmistry, phrenology and other techniques which Professor Eysenck says he puts into the general category of 'rubbish'.

Falsification

It was pointed out earlier that because there was no obvious logic to biodata that such questionnaires were difficult to falsify. There has, however, been evidence that selectors — usually field managers provided with the questionnaire designed to screen out likely failures — often guided their favourite candidates into giving the 'right' answers.

One method used to reduce fakability was to tell those completing the form that it included a lie-detection scale — which in fact it didn't. Experimental evidence suggests that people fake less when informed that a lie scale exists.

Unfair discrimination

Designers of biodata questionnaires will be aware of the law on matters of discrimination on the basis of sex or race. However, while the questionnaire may exclude direct questions on age or sex, many other questions on seemingly innocent characteristics may have an association with areas of prejudice — especially on the matter of colour. The address, for example, can discriminate in a relatively subtle way. There will be far fewer black candidates from the smarter London suburbs than from Brixton or Southall. Moreover, many items in biodata questionnaires are related to social class. For example, those on house ownership, car ownership and parents' occupations give clear clues to social class or at least financial worth. And, in both the United States and the United Kingdom, being non-white tends to mean being poor.

Conclusion

In summary, biodata appears to be a valuable and relatively inexpensive method of judging people for jobs. The questionnaires are not as readily fakable as personality tests and the validity can be readily demonstrated. Yet, there could be criticism: their technique could be seen as secretive and illogical. Personnel managers could, for example, have a hard time justifying to a television interviewer or an investigative journalist the making of employment decisions on seemingly arbitrary factors such as 'mother's education' or 'the number of guests who attended the wedding reception'. The fact that examined scientifically and statistically biodata is far superior to the interview may not carry great weight!

Further reading

Aiken, L.R. *Psychological Testing and Assessment*, 6th edn, Allyn & Bacon, Boston, 1988.

Beatty, R. W. and Schneier, C. E. *Personnel Administration: An Experimental Skill-building Approach*, Addison-Wesley, Reading, MA, 1977.

Cook, M. *Personality Selection and Productivity*, John Wiley, Chichester, 1988.

Cooper, C. L. and Robertson, I.T. (eds). *Industrial Review of Industrial and Organisational Psychology*, John Wiley, Chichester, 1986.

Dreher, G.F. and Sackett, P.R. (eds). *Perspectives on Employee Staffing and Selection*, Irwin, IL, 1983.

Dunnette, M.D. (ed.). *Handbook of Industrial and Organisational Psychology*, Rand McNally, Chicago, Illinois, 1976.

Guion, R.M., *Personnel Testing*, McGraw-Hill, New York, 1965.

The ability to learn

The ability to discern relationships

The ability to solve problems

Chapter 7
The Psychological Assessment

The psychological assessment of individuals is carried out for a range of purposes such as occupational guidance, counselling, career development, assessment of management potential and assessment for appointment to a specific role in an organisation.

The underlying assumptions

The psychologist's approach to judging people is based on three main assumptions:

- that certain personal characteristics are stable, and subject to measurement;
- that these can best be 'measured' by a combination of techniques;
- that the training and experience of the psychologist makes him best equipped to use these techniques.

The techniques include different kinds of interviews and a range of 'tests'. (This term covers questionnaires, etc, to which there are no right and wrong answers, as well as intelligence and aptitude tests.)

Characteristics measured and instruments used

Intelligence

One of the classical, and useful, models of the structure of human abilities poses that there is a general factor that is present in everyone to a greater or lesser degree. Those who have it to a very high degree are described as geniuses or intellectually brilliant; at the lower end of the scale are those who might be called dull or moronic. This factor is the ability to learn, the ability to discern relationships, the ability to solve problems, and it is commonly called intelligence or general ability. (The term 'IQ' has, through popular usage, become more or less synonymous.) It is something that can be measured by the most highly developed of the psychologist's tools: the intelligence test.

The history of intelligence testing goes back much further than many people appreciate. It could be said to have started soon after the middle of the nineteenth century with the work of Galton, whose interest in heredity — and especially in the inheritance of intellectual ability — led him to devise methods of measuring individual differences and to provide quantified data; Galton established the first psychometric laboratory in the 1880s.

The historical background is complex, but the important result is that today psychologists have at their disposal tests of intelligence which are both valid and reliable. That is, they measure what they claim to measure and they do so consistently. Accepting that intelligence exists and can be measured, is it of importance.

Intelligence, as defined by psychologists, is not necessarily accompanied by originality or by 'common sense'; and almost always intelligence test results need to be used not in isolation but in the context of information about attainments, personality, motivation, etc. However, the fact that intelligence tests do not measure or, indeed, give any information about these other characteristics, is no reason for rejecting them. They are still useful measures of potential; as Eysenck said:

We make use of a hammer in spite of the fact that we cannot use it as a saw or for measuring the strength of an electrical current; it is difficult to see why we should reject intelligence tests because they measure intelligence rather than various other qualities which may also be important.

How well does the average interviewer assess a candidate's inteligence? It is a common finding that most interviewers do it badly, but with great confidence: a dangerous combination. While it is relatively easy — and justifiable — to conclude that a man or woman with a first-class degree in mathematics and a Fellowship of the Royal Society is 'bright', what of the person with limited education: how able is he? Many of the apparent signs are misleading: the lively, outgoing conversationalist is generally rated higher than the shy introvert; the highly-educated person is rated as cleverer than the one who may not have had the same educational opportunities; a successful business record is taken at its face value; even the person who wears glasses may be judged to be more intelligent than the one who does not.

The psychologist aims to discover not only how intelligent a person is but how effectively he or she applies his or her basic ability in various contexts. Many relevant tests are available (see Chapter 5) Some involve the manipulation of numbers, some call for reasoning in a purely verbal framework. Some mean working under pressure of time; in others the individual can work at his own pace. Some consist of concrete, clearly-defined problems and provide all the facts needed for their solution. More subtle tests ask the subject to consider non-factual issues: to weigh abstract arguments, for example, or to identify logical errors in propositions put to him. (The man who deals incisively and accurately with concrete problems sometimes falls back on his intuition, on his personal feelings, or on preconceived views when confronted with problems that are less black and white.)

Given the definition outlined above — the ability to discern relationships and solve problems — the common-sense answer to the question of whether the assessment of intelligence is of importance must be 'yes'. Indeed, in career guidance, much of the emphasis has moved from aptitude testing to interest and ability testing. That is, batteries of tests designed to identify qualities required for a brain surgeon, a salesman, chimney sweep, etc. are now rarely used. Today the psychologist will be more concerned to assess the range and depths of interests of the individual and the intellectual potential. The latter provides guidance as to the level at which the person should aim. To use a crude example, should the pattern of interests suggest the field of medicine, then the counsellor may have to decide whether the person should be advised to become a highly-specialised doctor or any one of the range of positions through nursing and other medical auxiliary work to the humbler positions of ward orderly and hospital porter.

Similar use of the knowledge of the intellectual level of the individual can be of help in career development and the establishment of management potential. If, to simplify matters, we limit the discussion of psychological assessment to the evaluation of managers then we can move on and provide evidence to support (or otherwise) the common-sense view that some knowledge of the intellectual capacity of the individual is important. Numbers of studies have shown positive correlations between intelligence level and management effectiveness. (This should not suggest that intelligence is the only quality required, nor that all intelligent people can be effective managers.) It appears, however, to be *necessary* but certainly not *sufficient*. There is also evidence that successful executives are more logical and objective than are the less successful ones.

Personality

The assessor, layman or psychologist, usually aims to assess the complex matter of personality by considering more or less clearly-defined separate aspects, or factors, and then coming to an integrated view of the individual. Personality factors which commonly appear on selectors' lists of characteristics to be assessed include:

1. Emotional toughness and resilience
2. Self-confidence and decisiveness
3. Readiness to work hard/activity level
4. Flexibility: capacity to adapt to change, to turn readily from one matter to another
5. Assertiveness/dominance
6. Independence
7. Friendliness/sociability
8. Sensitivity to others' feelings
9. Objectivity

Again research findings support the view that such factors are relevant to management success.

In assessing these traits the layman has to rely on the information he gets from an interview, or a series of interviews, from 'references' given by, for example, previous employers, and on his observations of the person's behaviour.* Careful interviewing, in particular, can provide valuable data — and there is evidence that trained interviewers make more accurate judgements of people than untrained interviewers. Even so, the majority of psychologists use additional

---

* The 'stress interview' is sometimes employed, more by lay interviewers than by psychologists, in an attempt to judge how a person will behave under pressure. The candidate is often treated with deliberate rudeness, or even aggression, and his response to this is noted by the interviewer. The author believes that this is neither a socially acceptable technique nor necessarily a valid one: the way an individual may behave when subjected to artificial stress can be very different from his reaction to real-life pressures. (There would appear to be almost no published work providing evidence for the validity of the stress interview.)

Emotional toughness and resilience

Self-confidence and decisiveness

Readiness to work hard/activity level

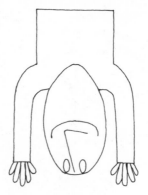

Flexibility

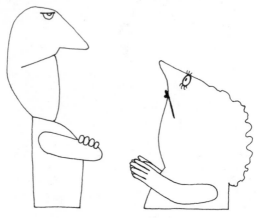

Assertiveness/dominance

Independence

Friendliness/sociability

Sensitivity to others' feelings

Objectivity

tools such as intelligence tests and personality questionnaires. Indeed, some psychologists, concerned to be as objective as possible, rely almost exclusively on such instruments in making their assessments of personal traits. But most would probably agree with Cattell and Kline:

We should not advocate in either selection or guidance the mechanical use of these procedures (personality questionnaires such as Cattell's 16PF). This is because the reliabilty and validity of the tests, although good, is not perfect, so that in the individual case there is room for error ... we would always want to ensure that the results were appropriate by careful interviewing.

Cattell and Kline go on to say: 'This is not to elevate the interview above tests but simply to recognise that it can provide a useful amplification for test scores.'

Most conventional personality questionnaires either invite the respondent to agree or disagree with a series of statements about the way he behaves/feels/believes or ask him more direct questions about such things. There is now considerable evidence that in some situations (such as that of being an applicant for a job) people may be motivated — consciously or unconsciously — to present themselves in what they see as a favourable light. Many psychologists therefore tend to be wary of placing undue weight on the results of such question- naires in the selection context. But even when they present a picture which is consistent with all other evidence, the psychologist still has, at times, a difficult task in interpreting them. There can be almost countless permutations of factors. Consider the possibilities with only three factors: intelligence, stability and introversion. Intelligent, stable, introvert; intelligent, unstable, introvert; intelligent, unstable, extra- vert; less intelligent, unstable, extravert; and so on ...; all very different types of people. And the psychologist may be having to consider permutations of as many as 20 factors (and varying levels of each factor: people are not simply either introvert or extravert but at some point on a scale with introversion at one extreme and extraversion at the other).

Interpretations of such data calls for a sound understanding of personality theory and much experience. And even greater experience and psychological insight is needed for a second group of personality tests, the 'projectives'. In these the individual may be shown a series of pictures (or the well-known Rorschach ink blots, see Figure 16) and

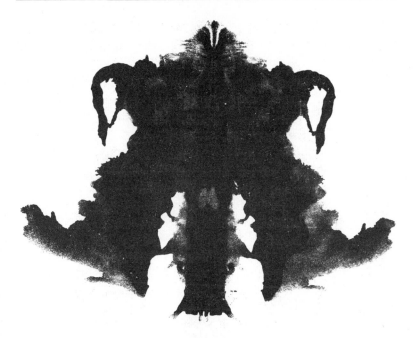

Figure 16 A Rorschach ink blot

asked to produce stories about them; perhaps more commonly, he may be presented with the beginnings of a series of sentences and asked to complete them. The hypothesis is that the person's responses reflect aspects of his personality; someone who ends a sentence beginning 'Often I ...' with 'feel frightened and inadequate' contrasts strongly with the one who puts 'think there are no limits to what I can achieve'. These are extreme examples; but a sensitive psychologist can often learn a great deal from less obvious responses.

A management assessment programme

The following procedure, which is that followed by the author, is fairly typical of the way industrial psychologists go about assessing managers, or potential managers.

The individual, who may be a short-listed external candidate for a senior position, an internal candidate for a specific promotion, or a young manager being considered for an expensive training course, is invited by the company concerned to spend the best part of a day with an outside professional adviser. To reduce the air of mystery he is usually given in advance some details of what will happen. (Some companies have printed leaflets outlining the procedure and explaining why they use it, what they expect to get out of it, and what the individual concerned can expect to get from it in the way of subsequent 'feedback'.) The first item on the programme is always a preliminary informal talk with the psychologist. This has two functions: first, to make sure that the person knows what the day's programme is going to consist of and that he or she understands the objectives of the whole exercise; secondly, to reduce any tension. The psychologist's aim is to get across to the person that he is not going to be subjected to such experiences as 'stress interviews' and that there is no question of his passing or failing on the various paper-and-pencil tests he will be doing. The person then spends some hours working on the tests; he or she also has an extensive interview with the psychologist.

The interview, which is central to the programme, is conducted as an informal, unstructured discussion; there are no questions probing into private matters. The person is asked in essence to describe his life history: a task which, after possibly a little initial embarrassment, most people enjoy.

If there is a technique involved in this kind of interviewing it is a technique of listening, of stopping oneself from interrupting, of tolerating pauses while the person thinks about how to describe what happened next, of asking open-ended questions and subtly encouraging him or her to talk freely (see Chapter 4). In this kind of interview, attitudes and opinions will inevitably emerge as well as facts; and the interviewer is listening for the former as well as for evidence of recurring themes or patterns of behaviour in the life history. (The man who has consistently made major decisions for himself in the past is likely to continue to do so in the future; the man who has always led an essentially solitary life is unlikely to change into a highly gregarious person, even if his personality test results suggest that that is how he would like to see himself.)

At the end of the day, all the data are assembled: test scores, profiles from personality questionnaires, responses to projective tests, interview findings, and anything else judged relevant. (The last may include observations of unusually nervous or apologetic or aggressive behaviour during the day.) In making his judgements, the aim of the psychologist is to construct a 'model' (inevitably an over-simplified one) of the person which can then be used to predict how he will behave at work. The report eventually produced will not go into the causes of any behaviour thus predicted; it may say *'He will be a cautious decision-maker'*, but it will not say *'Because he had acute fears of falling at an early age he has been left with a strong need to avoid risk and so will be a cautious decision-maker'*; it may say *'He is drivingly ambitious'*, but it will not go on to say *'in compensation for feelings of inferiority resulting from a deprived background'*. The report to the company describes the person's style in three main areas of functioning.

1. Intellectual effectiveness

- Basic intellectual capacity (compared with other managers)
- Quick learner?
- Conceptual thinker?
- Numeracy?
- Verbal skills: ability to communicate in speech and writing?
- An objective thinker? or much influenced by his emotions?
- Able to produce original ideas? Imaginative? Strictly conventional?

2. Work style

- Generalist or detail-minded?
- Sense of priorities?
- Decision-making approach: impulsive? cautious? slow? confident?
- Strategist — long-term planner? Tactician?
- Energetic? Highly restrained? Not vigorous but efficient?
- Tolerance for pressure: stable? high risk?
- Reaction to emergencies: calm? flustered?
- Ambitions: how important to him? will he sacrifice other interests? are his aims realistic?
- Flexibility: can he handle a number of tasks in parallel?
- Adaptability: can he adjust to different environments?

3. Personal relationships

- General impact: what first impression does he make?
- Does he have 'presence'?

- What will be his impact on people outside the organisation?
- Relationships with boss: frank? amenable? stubborn? loyal?
- Relationships with peers: friendly? co-operative? tolerant? a team person? highly competitive? a loner?
- Relationships with subordinates: domineering? protective? decisive? sensitive? willing to delegate?
- Relationships with outsiders: confident? careful? disdainful? courteous?

A summary at the end of the report includes lists of what appear to be the person's major assets and main limitations in relation to the needs of a particular job. A recommendation may be made about the suitability of his personal characteristics for a specific position (it is obviously not the psychologist's job to assess his technical qualifications or his work experience). Alternatively, a general assessment of his potential may be given.

The report also usually contains a short section pointing to any major developmental needs and suggesting specific ways of meeting these, such as particular training courses or reading programmes. It may also include advice for the individual's boss on the style of management he is likely to respond to. (Does he need a good deal of support and encouragement? or close control? or to be given a degree of independence?)

Feedback

Some psychologists consider that an offer of 'feedback', a discussion of the main findings with the 'candidate' is almost an ethical requirement: the individual is entitled to this talk with the psychologist — to know what has been said about him. In a typical feedback session the psychologist will not only advise the person on how to capitalise on his strengths but will also give him some counselling on how he might correct, or compensate for, or come to terms with, his weaknesses. Candidates almost invariably welcome this open 'warts and all' discussion, and the knowledge that they are entitled to it gives the whole assessment procedure a positive appeal. Managers already established in their organisations often ask to have a psychological assessment so that they will have more evidence to help them think about, and plan, their careers.

The future

There is widespread evidence of the growth in the use of psychological assessments and that this development appears to be continuing. John Handyside reports that when he was looking for external psychologists to carry out assessments for Standard Telephones and Cables plc (STC), he was hard put to find more than 'two or three'. Even around 1980 there were only 10 or 12 established practices. A recent survey (1989) conducted by Dr Richard Ford produced a list of between 60 and 70 practices — and Ford makes no claim for this as a comprehensive list. Companies frequently use outside assessors both to evaluate the people on the short-list of external candidates recruited for a vacant position, to consider internal candidates for promotion or transfer, and for 'general evaluation'. That is, employees are invited to go through an assessment programme to help the company identify their potential and plan their future careers. Many companies have their internal resources but others believe in using the external assessor who they judge may have greater objectivity and where, in particular there will be no fear of political influences. (An internal assessor could have some interest in just who was recommended for promotion and who not; this would rarely be a matter of concern for the external consultant.) Companies such as Lucas, Boots, Abbey Life, British Airways and many others make regular use of psychological assessment when considering senior appointments. Moreover, the growth is beyond the straightforward assessment of individuals and into the field of 'management audit' in which a company decides to take stock of their human resources. They want answers to such questions as 'Just what talent have we available to us now? and 'What potential do we have for the future?' Also, recruitment consultants (including executive search consultants — the 'headhunters') are now using psychologists not only to help clients with assessment but also to monitor the quality of their own activities. The psychological assessors in turn are on the outlook for new or at least more refined instruments.

Alas, psychological tests are not developing rapidly. Even the most imaginative and brilliant of new approaches has to be tested and validated before it can be put into practice. Lay people, taking their initial look at psychological tests, often comment on the early date of publication of some of the instruments. The fact is that the more data collected on a test the more valuable it is likely to be. Indeed, should a consultant boast that his tests are new, the buyer should be properly sceptical.

There are two main methods of assessing the validity of a test — that is, assessing the degree to which it measures what it purports to measure. The first is 'concurrent validity': this relates the scores on tests to the competence of people doing the job. The second is 'predictive validity' in which the aim is to determine the extent scores predict actual performance. This 'longitudinal' method can only be carried out over an extended period of time. For example, in 'concurrent validity' scores on tests of mechanical aptitude would be related to the evaluated skills of a group of working mechanics; in 'predictive validity' the measure would be of which candidates will succeed (and how well) in becoming a mechanic. 'Predictive validity' — the one which takes time — is the statistic preferred by many.

Conclusion

In summary, while there is undoubted growth in the field of psychological assessment, the development of instruments is still relatively and, as suggested above, almost inevitably slow. While Saville & Holdsworth, for example, have introduced a whole range of new tests, even these are developments of existing knowledge rather than a breakthrough. Moreover, although the computer can (and does) contribute by marking tests swiftly and carrying out rapid and complicated statistical analyses the adaptive computer — the one which will learn from the subject — is far from widespread. Indeed, at the time of writing, its use was confined to a few advanced research laboratories. Slightly more widespread is the occasional program which enables the computer to write a narrative report. As discussed, however, these are not yet satisfactory.

The indications are that the best results will still be gained from a psychologist who is a competent interviewer working with instruments with which he is familiar. If he can add some of the qualities of the gifted judge (discussed in Chapter 9) so much the better. In the opinion of the author assessment, particularly at the top level, depends very considerably on the judgement of the assessor. At lower levels the selection of salesmen, engineering apprentices, clerks, etc. can be carried out very satisfactorily with the use of the appropriate tests (see Chapter 5).

Further reading

Albright, L.E., Glennon, J.R. and Smith, W.J. *The Use of Psychological Tests in Industry*, Scandinavian University Books, Copenhagen, 1963.

Anstey, E. *An Introduction to Selection Interviewing*, HMSO, London, 1977.

Campbell, J.P., Dunnette, M.D., Lawler, E.E. and Weick, K.E. *Managerial Behaviour, Performance and Effectiveness*, McGraw-Hill, New York, 1970.

Cattell, R.B. and Kline, P. *The Scientific Analysis of Personality and Motivation*, Academic Press, London, 1977.

Cook, M. *Personnel Selection and Productivity*, John Wiley, Chichester, 1988.

Cronback, L.J. *Essentials of Psychological Testing*, Harper & Row, New York, 1959.

Eysenck, H.J. *Uses and Abuses of Psychology*, Penguin, Harmondsworth, 1953.

Ghiselli, E.E. *Explorations in Managerial Talent*, Goodyear, California, 1971.

Ghiselli, E.E. *The Validity of Occupational Aptitude Tests*, John Wiley, New York, 1966.

Guion, R.M. *Personnel Testing*, McGraw-Hill, New York, 1965.

Mackenzie Davey, D. and Harris, M. *Judging People*, McGraw-Hill, London, 1982.

Mackenzie Davey, D. and McDonnell, P. *How to Interview*, British Institute of Management, London, 1975.

McClelland, D.C. *The Achieving Society*, Irvington, New York, 1976.

Muller, H. *'The search for the qualities essential to advancement in a large industrial group: An exploratory study'* (anon. company), The Hague, 1970.

Smith, M. and Robertson, I.T. *The Theory and Practice of Systematic Staff Selection*, Macmillan, London, 1986.

Vernon, P.E. *Personality Assessment*, Methuen, London, 1964.

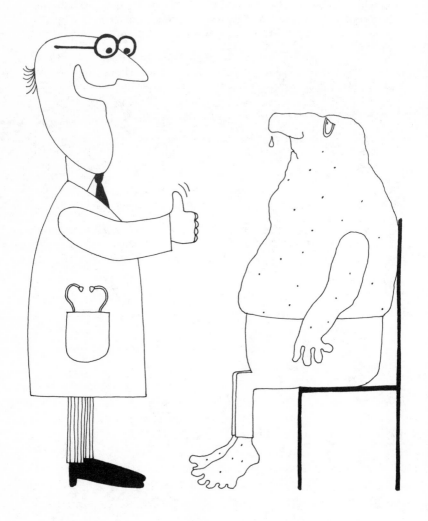

The ability to lie convincingly

Chapter 8
Assessment Centres

The assessment centre is, perhaps, the most elaborate of the conventional techniques used to judge people. Typically the process will take at least a full day — and often two or even more days. The assessment is carried out by a team of judges using a range of techniques almost always including interviews, psychological tests, group discussions, simulation exercises and peer ratings. Assessment centres are primarily used for management selection but can also be used for career development and/or the identification of potential.

Current assessment centres are direct developments of the War Office Selection Boards (WOSBs) and the post-war Civil Service Selection Boards (CSSBs). These were far more elaborate than the selection programmes they replaced (often no more than an interview and, perhaps, an essay) involving candidates and assessors in several days of their time.

Similar techniques were developed by the Office of Strategic Services in the United States. These initially, were concerned with the selection of agents and, in consequence, the emphasis was on techniques believed to be essential for secrecy work. For example, during the assessment, each candidate was required to pretend to be someone else — 'Someone who had been born where he wasn't, who had been educated in institutions other than those he had attended, who had been engaged in work or a profession not his own, and to have lived in a place that was not his true residence'. Psychologist Mark Cook comments that 'the OSS programme must be unique in regarding systematic lying as a virtue'. Yet it was designed to identify a skill in deception which could be of central importance. And, indeed, such a skill is not limited to spying. It can (as discussed in Chapter 3) be important in as respectable a profession as medicine. Readers may wish to reflect on other professions in which the ability to lie convincingly is important. Politics (of course), teaching, police work, and so on — and on!

One of the great post-war studies of assessment centres was conducted in American Telegraph and Telephone (AT&T). This programme included a business game, a leaderless group discussion, an 'in-basket' (in-tray) exercise, an extensive interview, an autobiographical essay, a personal history questionnaire, projective tests, personality inventories and high level intelligence testing. The original study assessed over 400 candidates who were followed up six or seven years later. The assessment centre ratings predicted success in management with a level of accuracy which far surpassed all earlier methods. This led to the development of centres on a large scale with AT&T alone having 50 centres assessing some 10,000 candidates a year.

One of the attractive exercises in the assessment centres is the in-tray exercise. In this, the candidate has to assume that he has just been appointed (or promoted) to a position in which he is faced with a full 'in-tray'. He is unable to make contact with his predecessor and has to judge for himself the importance and urgency of each item. The items might include notice of an impending strike in a major part of the organisation, a note from a secretary reminding the executive that the chairman's wedding anniversary falls on the following day and it has been customary for the department to send flowers to him and his wife. Other items may vary from the letter of resignation from a key employee to relatively trivial issues. (*'Mr Bloggins returned your call'*, *'Thank you for your donation to the Poppy fund'*, etc.) After dealing with the in-tray in the limited time allowed, the candidates can be interviewed about their proposed actions and asked to account for them. In at least one assessment centre the following dimensions are assessed from the candidate's performance on the in-tray exercise.

1. Oral communication skill
2. Written communication skill
3. Stress tolerance
4. Leadership
5. Sensitivity
6. Flexibility
7. Initiative
8. Planning and organisation
9. Delegation and control
10. Problem analysis
11. Judgement
12. Decisiveness
13. Reading and understanding

Oral communication skill

Written communication skill

Stress tolerance

Leadership

Sensitivity

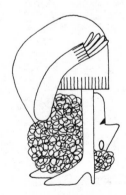

Flexibility

Initiative

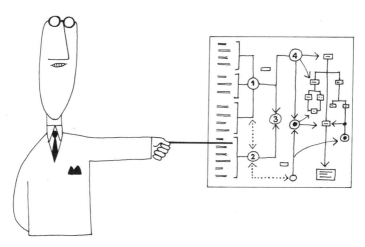

Planning and organisation

Delegation and control

Problem analysis

Judgement

Decisiveness

Reading and understanding

Another assessment centre exercise is the leaderless group discussion. In this the candidates are given a non-technical, controversial topic (should capital punishment be brought back? should there be random breath testing?), asked to discuss it and reach an agreed conclusion within a specified period of time. The discussion is observed and participants assessed on such issues as assertiveness, leadership quality, flexibility, political alertness, imagination, problem analysis, judgement, decisiveness, independence, etc. Clearly one danger of these exercises is extrapolating from insufficient evidence. (The fact that the candidate generated one constructive idea should not be taken as evidence of notable creativity.) Group discussions leave powerful impressions but these should not be considered in isolation. At the end of the candidate's participation in an assessment centre the assessors must spend a good deal of time evaluating *all* the evidence. (In some assessment centres the assessors spend more time evaluating the evidence than was spent gathering it.)

As well as leaderless group discussions there can be 'assigned leadership' exercises in which an individual is told, for example, that he is chairman of a committee and it is his objective to get agreement on a particular proposal.

There are also role-playing tasks such as dealing with an irate customer, admonishing a delinquent junior, counselling a disgruntled employee or considering a candidate for promotion.

There can also be team exercises in which one half of the group advocates a case and the other half takes the opposing viewpoint.

(Again, assessments are made on negotiating skill, team work, problem-solving ability etc.)

One cruel exercise developed by the Office of Strategic Studies involved a candidate building a simple structure from pegs, poles and blocks. He was given two 'assistants' and asked to build as many as possible in 10 minutes. The 'assistants' had, of course, been briefed — one to be passive and sluggish the other aggressive, quick to criticise, offering impractical suggestions and generally expressing dissatisfaction. The assistants were not permitted to disobey orders but would carry them out explicitly and literally.

A typical protocol is reproduced here to illustrate how the helpers turned the conversation into banter which could be exploited for purposes of personality assessment.

STAFF MEMBER [*calling toward the barn*]: Can you come out here and help this man for a few minutes?

BUSTER AND KIPPY: Sure, we'll be right out.

STAFF MEMBER: OK, Slim, these are your men. They will be your helpers. You have ten minutes.

SLIM: Do you men know anything about building this thing?

BUSTER: Well, I dunno, I've seen people working here. What is it you want done?

SLIM: Well, we have got to build a cube like this and we only have a short time in which to do it, so I'll ask you men to pay attention to what I have to say. I'll tell you what to do and you will do it. OK?

BUSTER: Sure, sure, anything you say, Boss.

SLIM: Fine. Now we are going to build a cube like this with five-foot poles for the uprights and seven-foot poles for the diagonals, and use the blocks for the corners. So first we must build the corners by putting a half block and a whole block together like this and cinching them with a peg. Do you see how it is done?

BUSTER: Sure, sure.

SLIM: Well, let's get going.

BUSTER: Well, what is it you want done, exactly? What do I do first?

SLIM: Well, first put some corners together — let's see, we need four on the bottom and four topside — yes, we need eight corners. You make eight of these corners and be sure that you pin them like this one.

BUSTER: You mean we both make eight corners or just one of us?

SLIM: You each make four of them.

BUSTER: Well, if we do that, we will have more than eight because you already have one made there. Do you want eight altogether or nine altogether?

SLIM: Well, it doesn't matter. You each make four of these, and hurry.

BUSTER: OK, OK.

KIPPY: What cha'in, the Navy? You look like one of them curly-headed Navy boys all the girls are after. What cha'in, the Navy?

[*And so on.*]

This situation so distressed most candidates that not even *one* construction was ever, in the history of the exercise, completed in the allotted time!

At the end of the exercises the assessors confer, often, as indicated, at great length, to evaluate the available evidence and make recommendations about the candidates.

The validity of assessment centres

Although there has been continuing work on assessment centres over many years, the three main areas of research remain the War Office Selection Boards and Civil Service Selection Boards in the United Kingdom and the AT & T researchers in the United States. These provide weighty evidence that assessment centres can provide better forcasts of future performance than most other far more widely-used techniques. But, as Bernard Ungerson pointed out as long ago as 1974,

All these were composed of highly trained, full-time professional members and all used pencil and paper tests as well as subjective judgemental procedures. It is quite fallacious to assume that similar validities can be achieved by programmes using non-specialists, with brief training and without the contribution of pencil and paper tests. Such programmes cannot 'ride on the back' of the results achieved by WOSB and AT & T.

Unfortunately superficial inspection does not readily discriminate between the 'real' assessment centre and a procedure that looks good and which, perhaps, the vendors are describing as almost infallible. The attempt, however, to economise is great because of the admittedly high expense of a well-run assessment centre. (If these are to be properly costed and, for example, the time spent in preparing the programme and time spent by the assessor included in the calculation, the final figure can be frighteningly high.) Even if a standard package is used, the cost may well be £5000 per candidate. If new exercises are designed for each programme the cost will, of course, be substantially higher. But recruitment costs are also high: the cost of appointing a senior executive who may have been evaluated on no more than an interview and track record can be £20,000.

'Track record' is not, of course, an insignificant issue. Indeed, it can be of central importance. The difficulty, however, is that many people recruited for positions in which they will have greater responsibility, require to deal with more complex problems, than they had in the past. Thus, although a track record provides sound evidence of what a candidate *has* done and what he *can* do, it may be less than perfect in predicting what he *will* do in different circumstances in the future. In a review of assessment centres, Clive Fletcher also points out that the favourable findings of, for example, the AT & T assessment centre 'do not automatically confirm validity on any such centre that is set up'. And, in summary, while he expresses admiration for assessment-centre technique he accepts that, especially where 'candidates are drawn from the existing work force, there may be more effective ways of using information about them which could produce comparable results at less expense'. In a thorough survey of selection methods Paul M. Muchinsky of the Industrial Relations Centre, Iowa State University, attempted to evaluate a number of techniques on four factors.

I. Validity

The capacity of the predictor to forecast accurately criterion performance.

2. Fairness

The legal ramifications of discrimination and bias on such factors as sex, race, age, etc.

3. Applicability

The extent to which the selected method can be applied across the full range of job and applicant types. Some methods have wide applicability and are suited for a diverse range of people in jobs; others have far more limited use.

4. Cost

Muchinsky admits that it is difficult to arrive at a precise cost figure and warns that this is an area that has been neglected by psychologists who have been far more concerned with validity and fairness.

Muchinsky admits his findings are over-simplified but they appear to be fair-minded and are expressed in simple terms. Chapter 10 discusses some further comparisons of the methods of judgements shown in Table 5.

Table 5 Assessment of personnel selection methods along four evaluative standards

Test	Validity	Fairness	Applicability	Cost
Intelligence tests	Moderate	Moderate	High	Low
Aptitude and ability tests	Moderate	High	Moderate	Low
Personality and interests tests	Moderate	High	Low	Moderate
Interviews	Low	Moderate	High	Moderate
Biographical information	High	Moderate	High	Low
Assessment-centre evaluations	High	High	Low	High

Source: *International Review of Industrial and Organisational Psychology,* 1986.

Designing an assessment centre

All serious commentators on the assessment centre emphasise the need for a fully professional programme if the high validity of the best programmes is to be achieved. First, the programme needs to be designed and directed by a professional. This will be a psychologist not only experienced in all the elements contributing to an assessment centre but to the operation of the whole programme.

Essential elements

1. Psychological tests. As has been indicated previously, it is absurd to guess at the strength of characteristics which can be measured accurately and objectively using psychological tests. Thus a professional assessment centre will use tests to evaluate general intelligence and other intellectual activities relevant to the purpose of the programme. In the evaluation of managers, for example, this is likely to include tests of verbal and numerical ability, of logical skills and probably some assessment of imagination or creativity.

2. Individual interviews. Assessors should be trained in how to interview either in the relatively subtle unstructured interview or the easier-to-use but less-flexible structured or 'behaviour description' interview. It can be difficult to persuade senior executives who are likely to be the assessors that they may need training in something they have been 'doing all their lives'. Yet, the massive evidence to support the view that the untrained interviewer is an unreliable judge cannot be overlooked.

3. Group discussions. Here again the assessors need training. They have to learn to recognise that this is a matter of evaluating social interaction and not intellectual efficiency. One is, for example, far more concerned with how well an individual's contributions are received than how valuable they are. (As indicated above there are better ways of evaluating intelligence than observing a group discussion.) It can, for example, be useful to present assessors with a list of clearly defined characteristics on which they should base an evaluation after observing a discussion. They should not be left to say, '*I like Miss K — I think there is far more to her than meets the eye*'.

Important elements

1. Design of the 'in-tray' exercises. Ideally this should be varied for purposes of security: if the contents of the in-tray were known to candidates in advance it could invalidate the exercise. Another aspect of in-tray exercise design is gaining agreement between assessors on which *are* the more important decisions and which can be postponed.

2. Simulation exercises. It is important that the role is given as much reality as is possible. Candidates for the position of senior foreman should not be asked to play the role of the British Ambassador in Washington.

An admirable study of an assessment centre can be found. *The Method II System of Selection* — the report of a Committee of Inquiry chaired by JGW Davis and published by HMSO in 1969. A summary of the same programme will be found in the *Report of the Committee on the Selection Procedure for the Recruitment of Administrative Trainees* prepared by a committee under the chairmanship of Dr FH Allan, published by the Civil Service Commission in 1979. The work of Douglas Bray also deserves attention especially *Formative Years in Business: A Long term AT & T Study of Managerial Lives.*

Further reading

Bray, W., Campbell, R.J. and Grant, D.L. *Formative Years in Business: A Long Term AT & T Study of Managerial Lives,* John Wiley, New York, London, 1974.

Campbell, J.P. *et al., Managerial Behaviour, Performance, and Effectiveness,* McGraw-Hill, New York, 1970.

Cook. M. *Personality Selection and Productivity,* John Wiley, Chichester, 1988.

HMSO. *The Method II System of Selection* [for the administrative class of the Home Civil Service]: *Report of the Committee of Inquiry* 1969. HMSO, London, 1969.

Jaffe, C.L. *Effective Management Selection: The Analysis of Behaviour by Simulation Techniques,* Addison-Wesley, Reading, MA, London, 1971.

Jaffe, C.L. and Frank, F.D. *Interviews Conducted at Assessment Centres: A guide for Training Managers,* Kendall/Hunt, Dubuque, IO, 1976.

Keil, E.C. *Assessment Centres: A guide for Human Resource Management,* Addison-Wesley, Reading, MA, 1981.

Mackenzie Davey, D. and Harris, M. (eds.). *Judging People,* McGraw-Hill, London, 1982.

Moses, J.L. and Byham, W.C. *Applying the Assessment Centre Method,* Pergamon, New York, 1977.

The OSS Assessment Staff, *Assessment of Men,* Rinehart, New York, 1948.

Smith, M. and Robertson, I.T. *Systematic Staff Selection,* Macmillan, 1986.

Stewart, A. and Stewart, V. *Tomorrow's Managers Today: The Identification and Development of Management Potential,* 2nd edn, IPM, London, 1981.

Thorton, G.C. and Byham, W. C. *Assessment Centres and Managerial Performance,* Academic Press, New York, 1982.

Vernon, P. E. and Parry, J. B. *Personnel Selection in the British Forces,* University of London Press, 1949.

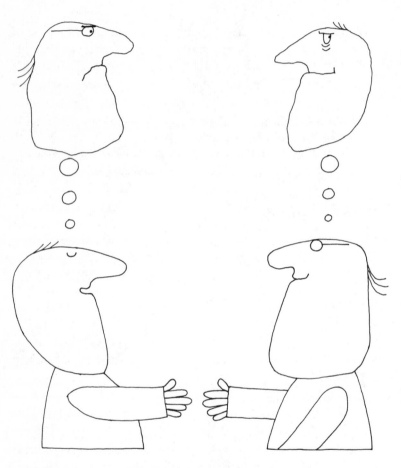

First impressions

Chapter 9
Intuitive Judgement

'People have always tried to judge others.' This was the opening sentence of Chapter 1 and over the following chapters we have discussed the various techniques and approaches adopted by people to increase their understanding of others. But, while we are constantly making judgements of others, most of us are not administering psychological tests, conducting formal interviews, studying handwriting or running assessment centres. Yet, we make judgements, often of the most sweeping kind on what most scientists would say was wholly insufficient evidence. And, while we make judgements with considerable confidence on first impressions most of us would also admit that we do not fully understand even the person closest to us. Indeed, it can be argued that no one person can completely understand another. Wives of thirty years' standing continue to surprise their husbands (and vice versa), children will astonish their parents and sometimes parents their children. None of these experiences, however, inhibits most people from making rapid and surprisingly confident first impression judgements.

First impressions

Two people meet for the first time. They discuss the weather, where they live, the latest news and perhaps the person who introduced them. After five minutes they will part without having revealed any information of a specifically personal nature. Nevertheless, each carries away an impression of the personality of the other. The first may think the second open, honest, amusing, intelligent and reliable; the second may think of the first that he is quiet, deep, not wholly to be trusted but yet possibly a useful friend. While these impressions are often strongly held — and surprisingly lasting — almost all the available evidence suggests that most of them are also wrong.

The remarkable speed and range of first judgements can be experienced by anyone: when next travelling on a bus or train look at a stranger for, say, three seconds then turn away. This is usually sufficient to arouse within the next half minute or so judgements not simply of sex, age and social class but also of such matters as

Wives continue to surprise their husbands

intelligence, sensitivity, friendliness, generosity, honesty, integrity and so on. Early experiments on extremely brief 'interviews' showed that there was often high agreement between judges — but little evidence of validity.

An experiment dealing with the validity of first impressions was carried out by Estes who published his results in 1937. This work has provided the basis for many replications and much of the work on 'intuitive' judgement over the subsequent fifty years. Estes used two short (two minute) films of behaviour of subjects whose personalities had been intensely studied by a group of twenty psychologists over a period of a year. In these films the subjects performed certain 'expressive' tasks (such as taking off their coat, tie and shirt; wrestling with an opponent; holding a lighted match for as long as possible, and building a house of playing cards). Thirty-seven judges, all psychiatric social workers, watched the films and were required to make ratings on the same traits as had been used by the psychologists. Studies of the findings showed that the ten best judges were uniformly better than the ten poorest judges for *all* variables and for *all* 'subjects' (the people shown in the film). The average of the ten best judges was 33 per cent higher than those of the ten poorest; and the best single judge was 62 per cent better than the poorest one. This would seem to lead to the conclusion that even in trained professionals the ability to 'sum up' people can be very different. That is, there appear to be gifted judges — and people who have little skill in assessing others.

A similar experiment was carried out recently but on this occasion using colour and sound film (as compared with Estes's silent black and white). Moreover, the situations were not structured but 'clips' were taken after long periods of informal filming. These 'clips', lasting between one and two minutes, were presented to an audience of some 400 managers who were required to make 'instant' diagnoses on a prepared format. The factors to be judged ranged through factual ones (age, job, socio-economic class, political inclinations) to more psychological factors (intelligence, introversion, stability, sensitivity, and the like). The complex analysis again produced evidence of gifted judges. Indeed, the highest scorers were almost uncannily accurate, again on all 'subjects' and all characteristics. Those at the bottom of the scale were worse than chance: had they ticked their judgement forms at random they would have done better! The next, and interesting, stage in experiments of the type described above is to try to identify the qualities of a good judge. And, so far, very little has been discovered.

Almost all experiments have shown that gifted judges are intelligent but there is no doubt that many intellectually powerful people can be hopelessly bad judges. Secondly, all gifted judges have met a lot of people. Plainly this suggests that older people are likely to be better than younger people but it is the experience with people rather than the number of years that appears to be important. (Thus, while it is more often the young who protest that their elders do not understand them, the indications are that the old have a very much better chance of understanding the young, than the young the old!)

Other factors which appear to be relevant are similarity: you are best able to judge people like yourself — perhaps because you can share more directly their thoughts, motives and feelings.

Most findings give no support to the concept of 'women's intuition'. Women are, it would seem, better at judging women but then men are better at judging men.

Sources of error

There is evidence that the main source of error is over-simplification. People who hold strong prejudices, for example, on nationality, race, accent, manners, dress etc., are likely to be over-influenced by these factors and so make wrong judgements.

Cook, whose rigorous scientific approach has made him critical of the methodology of many of the experiments described, questions whether the ability to judge is general or not. However, although he is alert to the many difficulties in the explorations of intuitive judgement, he regrets that interest in the problem has faded and believes that work in this undoubtedly important area ought to be continued. He has examined the research into the qualities of gifted judges which has ranged over age, sex, demographic variables (family size, social class, race etc.) intelligence, social skill and other qualities. His conclusions are by no means as simple as those discussed above but on the whole the findings lend some support to the view that age and intelligence are among the most important of the variables. In his latest book (*Personnel Selection and Productivity*) he appears to be becoming increasingly cynical of 'intuitive judgement' sardonically commenting that,

Personnel managers join an illustrious company: doctors, nurses, psychologists, radiologists, prison governers and social workers. All claim to make very sophisticated judgements; all show little evidence of actually doing so. Only one class of expert really does make complex configural decisions — the stockbroker.

Further reading

Argyle, M. *The Psychology of Interpersonal Behaviour*, 4th ed, Penguin, Harmondsworth, 1983.

Cook, M. *Interpersonal Perception*, Penguin, Harmondsworth, 1971.

Cook, M. *Perceiving Others*, Methuen, London, 1979.

Cook, M. (ed.). *Issues in Perception*, Methuen, London, 1984.

Cook, M. *Personnel Selection and Productivity*, John Wiley, Chichester, 1988.

Schneider, D.J., Hastorf, A.M. and Ellsworth, P.C. *Person Perception*, Addison-Wesley, London, 1979.

Chapter 10
The Future

How will people be judged in the future? Current indications are that, as in so many other areas, computers will have a very considerable influence. While this can be considerable — even spectacular — on relatively peripheral issues it may take a good deal longer before there are serious major changes. On the relatively superficial side the indications are that there will be far less contact between people in the judgement process. After all, computers can administer the range of tests discussed in Chapter 5 and the biodata discussed in Chapter 6.

Indeed tests can be administered with greater consistency, and scored with greater accuracy and with greater speed. Today, computers are capable of adapting to individual differences. It is quite possible to program a computer to test the intelligence with considerable subtlety. It can make an early diagnosis of the level of ability of the person being tested and move him onto more difficult or simpler paths as appropriate. Yet, such machines are almost never seen outside research laboratories.

Similarly, in the field of personality testing, machines already produce narrative reports. Currently these are crude documents, usually containing extensive repetition and a good deal of seeming contradiction. The immense subtlety of making judgements, as discussed in Chapter 7, in which a large number of variables have to be considered and interrelated will, for a long time, be beyond the capability of machines. Yet, it is possible to speculate that machines could be programed to deal with a mass of information from almost all the fields discussed and handle the data in an organised and systematic way. Even so, the conclusions may not be sound. And predicting whether a person who is tense, anxious and nervous will respond positively or negatively under pressure is still well beyond the relatively unsubtle judgements of a machine. Such a candidate could, for example, simply break down under the first serious pressure; alternatively he could respond by applying himself with greater intensity and application. The 'nervous energy', could be a source of high achievement.

There could, of course, be breakthroughs in totally unexpected fields. Some thirty years ago there was some evidence that electroen-cephalography (EEG) could provide evidence of differences of temperament (EEG involves recording the electrical activity of the brain); moreover, there was even some evidence that differences of intelligence could be detected from the objectively measured 'brain waves'. It is not beyond comprehension to assume that this branch of science could develop and find a practical implication in the assessment of people.

Chapter 11
A Final Word

It is often thought *de rigueur* that the author, after a survey of the type attempted in this book, should offer some evaluation of the techniques discussed. First offered here are the findings of a number of surveys. For example, Hunter and Hunter published an article in a psychological journal in 1984 on the validity and utility of alternative predictors of job performance. Some of their findings are published in Figure 17. These should be examined with Mark Cook's summaries given in Tables 6 and 7. In Table 6 he gives the conclusions of meta-analyses (meta-analysis is a technique in which the results of a number of separate researches, each one of them being relatively small, are combined to provide an overall unified figure). The figures for validity are based on the relationship between the test and the criteria used to measure the degree of success. Zero means no relationship; 1.00 would

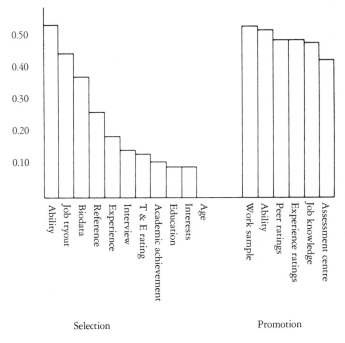

Figure 17 Estimates of the validity of various selection and promotion tests. Data from Hunter and Hunter (1984).

Table 6 Summary of meta-analyses of selection test validity

Selection test	Dunnette (1972)	Reilly and Chao (1982)	Vineberg and Joyner (1982)	Hunter and Hunter (1984)	Schmitt et al. (1984)
Graphology		'None'			
Interview	.0.16	0.23		0.14	
Reference check		0.17		0.26	
Peer ratings				0.49	0.43
Biodata	0.34	0.38	0.24	0.37	0.24
Cognitive ability	0.45			0.53	0.25
Perceptual ability	0.34				
Psychomotor ability	0.35				
Aptitude			0.28		0.27
Personality					
Interest inventory	0.03		0.13	0.10	0.15
Personality inventory	0.08				
Projective test		'Little'			
Assessment centre				0.43	0.41
Education	0.00		0.25	0.10	
Academic achievement		0.17		0.11	
T&E ratings				0.13	
Work sample				0.54	0.38
Job knowledge	0.51			0.48	
Job tryout	0.44				
Self-assessment		'Some'			
Physical test					0.32

Source: Cook, *Personnel Selection and Productivity*, 1988.

be a perfect correlation. It will be seen that the interview compares unfavourably with many other techniques — especially with ability testing and biodata, two of the techniques discussed in this book.

In Table 7 Cook summarises the range of selection methods against a number of criteria. From these he concludes,

Taking *validity* as the overriding consideration, there are six classes of test with high *validity*: peer ratings, biodata, ability tests, assessment centres, work sample tests and job knowledge tests. Three of these have very limited *generality*, which leaves biodata, ability tests and assessment centres.

However, statistical evidence rarely convinces: who really feels safer taking off in an airliner than driving his own car on familiar roads?

Thus, in spite of all the evidence about the lack of worth of the interview as an assessment technique there is virtually no selection procedure which does not use it. In the most recent survey of selection methods carried out by Marplan for Saville & Holdsworth Ltd (SHL) 300 heads of personnel of companies of 1000 or more employees were interviewed. The following is a brief summary of some of the findings.

- 66 per cent of companies said they had used ability tests in the last year in a serious way.
- 47 per cent of companies said they had used personality question-naires in a serious way in the last year. (These two findings combined to give a figure of 73 per cent of the companies using one or other or both type of psychological test.)
- 37 per cent used behavioural exercises of some sort. (That is, an assessment centre or some modification of that technique.)
- 3 per cent of the companies used graphology.
- 100 per cent of the companies used interviews.

What should the professional — the person who makes judgements of others as part of their paid job — do? Certainly examine the data provided above — and, of course, that provided in other surveys. The results do not show much variation.

Table 7 Summary assessment of ten selection tests by five criteria

Selection test	Validity	Cost	Practicality	Generality	Legality
Interview	Low	Medium/high	High	High	Untested
References	Moderate	Very low	High	High	A few doubts
Peer ratings	High	Very low	Very limited	Military only	Untested
Biodata	High	Medium	High	High	Some doubts
Ability	High	Low	High	High	Major doubts
Personality	Low	Low	Fair	?White-collar only	Untested
Assessment centre	High	Very high	Fair	Fairly	No problems
Work sample	High	High	High	Blue-collar only	No problems
Job knowledge	High	Low	High	Blue-collar only	Some doubts
Education	Low	Low	High	High	Major doubts

Source: Cook, *Personnel Selection and Productivity*, 1988.

The following are some guidelines which could help some people avoid some of the more serious mistakes in judging people.

1. Don't guess where you can measure. Intelligence, aptitude and achievement tests can all provide well-validated information on future performance. Even stability — the capacity for withstanding stress — can be assessed more effectively by test than by other means.
2. If you are going to interview, and you have not been trained, get trained. Or at least read some of the books listed at the end of Chapter 4.
3. Explore the techniques available — it is astonishing how many 'hi-tech' firms use 'low-tech' assessment techniques to evaluate their staff — and remember the difference between 'face validity' and 'real validity': statistical evidence, not appearance, is what is needed.
4. Stand back and examine your own feelings with objectivity. You could 'feel' there must be something in the firm handshake, the receding chin, the choice of clothes, the spidery, illegible handwriting, the preference of deep scarlet over pale blue — but what is the evidence? And remember your own anecdotal data have little scientific value (*'I knew that fellow was a wrong'un when I saw those suede shoes'.*)

The use of personality tests: a cautionary tale

Over thirty years ago Stagner gave a personality test to a group of managers (including personnel managers) and students. At the end of the exercise he gave each participant a profile. Asked to rate the description on a five point scale ranging from 'remarkably accurate' down to 'remarkably inaccurate' all groups rated them as 'remarkably accurate' or 'more right than wrong' — the top two of the five categories. What was then revealed was that Stagner had given every manager the same personality description. Of the groups, the personnel managers proved to be the most gullible. Next came other managers, and such scepticism as existed was found among students.

How did Stagner achieve these results? Largely by using a degree of flattery (*'You have a great deal of ability which you have not yet put to best use.'*), ambiguity (*'Sometimes you feel outgoing and sociable whereas at others you feel shy and reserved.'*) And there were also some mysterious items such as, '*You have had some difficulty with your sexual adjustment*'. Stagner was, of course, using the same technique as is used by the astrologers in popular papers and fortune tellers at the end of the pier.

Thus, users of personality tests should be highly suspicious of any salesman who offers a patter something like this: '*I can give you all the statistics, of course, but we all know what can be done with figures! I'll do better than that, I shall give you the test, score it, and give you the result: the description of your personality. If you find this accurate then you can see how valuable it would be in your selection process.*'

As indicated before, it is the statistics, the hard evidence, that one wants.

And what of the amateur who may be making (for him) equally momentous decisions — trusting a motor mechanic, believing (or not) a salesman, choosing a spouse, selecting a school for children (presumably based to a large degree on impressions of the teaching staff)? What can he do? At least he should be suspicious of his subjective judgement, whether from first impressions or based on discussion (an 'interview'). He should, as far as he is able look to the track record. How has he behaved in the past? The woman who believes that marriage will reform the charming, drunken, philanderer is almost certainly doomed to disappointment. All that is likely to happen is that the man becomes a married drunken philanderer. The salesman, however incoherent, who can offer a list of satisfied customers is to be trusted more than any fluent persuader who can offer no evidence of positive satisfaction with his product.

Alas, there appear to be no easy, short cut answers to judging people.

Glossary

Aptitude test
A test designed to measure capacity for achievement in a particular area. Thus mechanical aptitude, clerical aptitude etc. This instrument is designed to measure *potential* as opposed to *achievement* (*see* **Attainment test**).

Assessment centre
An eleborate technique used to judge people in which the assessment is carried out by a team of judges using a range of techniques such as interviews, psychological tests, group discussions, simulation exercises, etc. They are primarily used for management selection but have also been used for career development and the identification of potential.

Asthenic
One of the three body types used in Kretschmer's classification (*see* **Pyknic** *and also* **Athletic**). Asthenic (slender) types were believed to be predisposed to schizophrenia.

Astrology
The study of the influence of stars and planets on human personality and behaviour.

Athletic
One of the three body types in Kretschmer's classification (*see* **Asthenic** *and also* **Pyknic**). Athletic (muscular) types, according to Kretschmer, tended to be sane.

Attainment test
Test designed to show the level of knowledge or skill in a particular area in contrast to an aptitude test which measures the capacity for gaining skill and knowledge in a range of skills. School and similar examinations could be considered as attainment tests (*see* **Aptitude test**).

Biodata
A neologism from 'biographical data'. Biodata can be gathered in an

interview or questionnaire and is used to predict the behaviour of the candidate (*see* **Weighted Application Blank**).

Body Language
The communication through posture, gesture, facial expression which provides information on the feelings and even the character of the person observed.

Cerebrotonia
One of what was believed to be the three primary components of temperament – restrained, fearful, self-conscious (*see* **Somatotonia** *and also* **Visceratonia**).

Chirology
The term (preferred to 'palmistry') for the study of character based on interpretation of creases in the palm.

Dysplastic
An additional category used by Kretschmer to describe combinations of the three basic body types (**pyknic, asthenic** and **athletic**). Disproportioned.

Ectomorphic
Sheldon related three basic constitutional types to personality. (*see* **Endomorphic** *and also* **Mezomorphic**.) Ectomorphic (light boned) was related to **visceratonia** (loving, comfortable, sociable).

Endomorphic
Sheldon related three basic constitutional types to personality. (*see* **Ectomorphic** *and also* **Mezomorphic**.) Endomorphic (heavy, fat) related to **somatotonia** (vigorous, physical, adventurous).

Extraversion
Used to describe the personality whose interests are directed outwards. Such personalities gain satisfaction from their reaction to the physical and social environment, (*see* **Introversion**).

Graphology
The systematic study of handwriting to reveal the personality of the

writer. (Graphology is also used to detect forgery or to identify the writer of a particular document.)

Humours
Any of the four bodily fluids formerly thought to determine temperament and physique (blood, black bile, yellow bile, phlegm).

Intelligence
Psychologists remain unsatisfied with most definitions of intelligence but perhaps some of the least unsatisfactory are:

1. The ability to solve problems.
2. The ability to learn from experience.
3. The ability to relate seemingly disparate issues into a meaningful whole.
4. The ability to adapt successfully to the environment.
5. Cynically: 'what intelligence tests measure'.

Intelligence tests
A series of tasks which provide some measure of the individual's intellectual power.

IQ (intelligence quotient)
Originally the ratio of mental age to chronological age expressed as a percentage. Now used widely as a synonym for intelligence.

Introversion
Used to describe the type of personality in which the interest of the individual is in their own thoughts and feelings (*see* **Extraversion**).

Mezomorphic
Sheldon related three basic constitutional types to personality. (*see* **Ectomorphic** *and also* **Endomorphic**) Mezomorphic (strong, muscular) related to **cerebrotonia** (retrained, fearful, self-conscious).

Neurotic
A term used somewhat imprecisely for those whose behaviour tends to be unpredictable — people who appear to be suffering from a 'nervous' rather than a physical disorder.

Personality inventory

An instrument designed to give measures of various aspects of personality (often called 'traits'). In these the candidate responds by choosing one of a number of offered responses to a question or by saying 'Yes' or 'No' to a series of statements.

Personality test

A term covering all instruments designed to assess various aspects of temperament of personality (*see* **Personality inventory** *and also* **Projective test**).

Phrenology

Originally the science concerned with the location of function in the human brain and its reflection in the shape and size of the skull based on three assumptions.

i.   That there was a clear relationship between specific areas and particular mental functions.
ii. That the larger the area of the brain was the stronger the function.
iii. That the shape of the skull reflected the shape of the brain.

Because the first assumption is largely wrong, and the second two quite wrong, phrenology is now considered a pseudo science.

Physiognomy

The diagnosis of character, ability and attitudes from the face and facial expressions (*see* **Phrenology**).

Projective test

A test in which the candidate is asked to respond to some such stimulus as an ink blot (in the Rorschach Test) or pictures (as in Murray's Thermatic Apperception Test). The assumption is that people given the same stimulus will give different responses and these responses will reflect their different personalities. Although some attempt has been made to standardise the interpretation of responses most still call for extensive experience and a heavy reliance on intuition.

Psychological assessment

Typically a technique used to assess candidates in which a psychologist conducts an in-depth interview and uses a range of psychological tests. This results in a report assessing the candidate's suitability for a job or generally evaluating his potential or advising on career choice.

Pyknic
One of the three basic body types used in Kretschmer's classification (*see* **Asthenic** *and also* **Athletic**). Pyknic (stocky) types were believed to be predisposed to manic depression.

Reliability
In psychological testing reliability is used as a measure of the consistency of a test. That is, will a candidate achieve approximately the same score if tested a second and third time? (*see* **Validity**).

Somatotonia
One of what was believed to be the three primary components of temperament — vigorous, physical, adventurous (*see* **Cerebrotonia** *and also* **Visceratonia**).

Stable
Used to describe an individual who will remain reliable and consistent under stress. Non-neurotic (*see* **Unstable**).

Unstable
Used to describe an individual who tends to be erratic and unpredictable; neurotic; moved more by emotions than by logic.

Validity
A measure of whether a psychological test actually measures what it purports to measure. For example, the validity of a mechanical aptitude test would be the measure of how the results on tests compared with the actual performance subsequent to the test (*see* **Reliability**).

Visceratonia
One of what was believed to be the three primary components of temperament — loving, comfortable, sociable (*see* **Cerebrotonia** *and also* **Somatotonia**).

Weighted Application Blank

A biographical application form in which the items are allotted weights which have been shown to relate to behaviour. The weights are allotted from historical evidence. For example, in insurance, young drivers who drive sports cars are likely to have accidents. Thus insurers would give weight to those factors on the application form. The same system has been used to select employees (*see* **Biodata**).

Index